what's cooking
vegetarian

Jenny Stacey

p

This is a Parragon Publishing book
First published in 2004

Parragon Publishing
Queen Street House
4 Queen Street
Bath BA1 1HE
United Kingdom

ISBN: 1-40542-542-3

Printed in China

ACKNOWLEDGEMENTS

PHOTOGRAPHY: Andrew Sydenham

NOTE

This book uses imperial, metric, or US cups measurements. Follow the same units of measurement throughout;
do not mix imperial and metric. All spoon measurements are level: teaspoons are assumed to be 5 ml
and tablespoons are assumed to be 15 ml. Unless otherwise stated, milk is assumed to be whole, eggs and
individual vegetables such as potatoes are medium, and pepper is freshly ground black pepper.

The times given for each recipe are an approximate guide only. The preparation times may differ according to
the techniques used by different people and the cooking times may vary as a result of the type of oven used.
Ovens should be preheated to the specified temperature. If using a fan-assisted oven, check the manufacturer's
instructions for adjusting the time and temperature. The preparation times include chilling
and marinating times, where appropriate.

Recipes using raw or very lightly cooked eggs should be avoided by infants, the elderly,
pregnant women, convalescents, and anyone suffering from an illness.

contents

introduction

This book is designed to appeal to vegetarians, demi-vegetarians, and vegans alike. Its main aim is to dispel the myth that vegetarian food is brown, stodgy, and bland. When browsing through the recipes in this cookbook you will discover just how versatile, colorful, and flavorful a vegetarian diet can be.

Eating a balanced, nutritional diet is very important, and can be easily achieved by combining the recipes in this book when planning your meal, to include protein, carbohydrate, vitamins, minerals, and some fats. It is very important in any diet, but especially a vegetarian diet, that a good balance is achieved and that sufficient protein is eaten.

When cooking the recipes, feel free to substitute some ingredients to suit your specific diet, using soymilk for example in place of cow's milk, cream substitute instead of dairy cream and vegetable margarine in place of butter. A well-stocked pantry forms the backbone of any good cook's kitchen, and it is always useful to have plenty of basic foods ready to hand. Use the following information as a checklist when you need to replenish your stocks.

FLOUR

You will need all-purpose and self-rising flour if you want to make your own bread; and whole-wheat flour for using on its own or combining with white flour to make cakes and pastries. You can also keep rice flour and cornstarch for thickening sauces and to add to

cakes, cookies, and desserts. Buckwheat, chickpea, and soy flours can be bought from healthfood stores. These are useful for crêpes and for combining with other flours to add flavors and textures.

GRAINS

For rice, choose from long-grain, basmati, or Italian Arborio for making risotto; short-grain for desserts; and wild rice to add interest. Look out for fragrant Thai rice, jasmine rice, and combinations of different varieties to add color and texture to your dishes. Try to include some barley, millet, bulgur wheat, cornmeal, oats, semolina—including couscous, sago, and tapioca.

PASTA

Always make sure you have the basic lasagna sheets, tagliatelle, or fettuccine and spaghetti. Try spinach or tomato varieties for a change and sample some of the many fresh pastas now available in supermarkets. Better still, make your own—handrolling pasta can be very satisfying, or you can buy a special machine.

BEANS

Stock up on soybeans, haricot beans, red kidney beans, cannellini beans, chickpeas, lentils, split dried field peas, and lima beans. Buy dried beans for soaking and cooking yourself, or canned varieties for speed and convenience. Cook dried red and black kidney beans in boiling water for 15 minutes to destroy harmful toxins in the outer skin. Drain and rinse the beans, then let simmer until the beans are tender. Soybeans should be boiled for 1 hour, because they contain a substance that inhibits protein absorption.

SPICES & HERBS

There are many good spice mixtures available—try Cajun, Chinese five-spice, Indonesian piri-piri, and various curry blends. Try grinding your own spices with a mortar and pestle, or in a coffee mill. Although spices will keep well, don't leave them in the pantry

for too long, as they may lose strength. Buy small amounts as you need them. Fresh herbs are preferable to dried, but keep dried ones in stock as a back-up. Keep basics such as thyme, rosemary, and bay leaves.

CHILES

These come both fresh and dried, and in colors from green to yellow, orange, red, and brown. The "hotness" varies so use with caution, but as a guide the smaller they are the hotter they will be. The seeds are hottest and are usually discarded. When cutting chiles with bare hands do not touch your eyes; the juices will cause severe irritation. Chili powder should also be used sparingly. Check whether the powder is pure chili or a chili seasoning or blend, which should be milder. Chili sauces are used widely in Asian cooking, but again they vary in strength and sweetness.

NUTS & SEEDS

As well as adding protein, vitamins, and useful fats to the diet, nuts and seeds add important flavor and texture to vegetarian meals. To bring out the flavor of nuts and seeds, broil or roast them until lightly browned. Make sure that you keep a good supply of almonds, Brazil nuts, cashews, chestnuts (dried or canned), hazelnuts, peanuts, pecans, pistachios, pine nuts, and walnuts. Coconut—either creamed or dry unsweetened—is useful too. For your seed collection, have sesame, sunflower, pumpkin, and poppy.

DRIED FRUITS

Currants, raisins, golden raisins, dates, apples, apricots, figs, pears, peaches, prunes, papayas, mangoes, figs, bananas, and pineapples can all be purchased dried and can be used in lots of different recipes. When buying dried fruits, look for untreated varieties.

OILS & FATS

Oils are useful for adding subtle flavorings to foods. Use a light olive oil for cooking and extra virgin olive oil for salad dressings. Use corn oil as a good general-purpose oil and select one or two specialty oils to add character to different dishes. Sesame oil is wonderful in stir-fries while hazelnut and walnut oils are superb in salad dressings. Oils and fats contain the fat-soluble vitamins A, D, E, and K. Remember that all fats and oils are high in calories, and oils are higher in calories than butter or margarine—1 tablespoon of oil contains 134 calories, whereas 1 tablespoon of butter or margarine contains 110 calories. When you are using oil, it is a good idea to measure it—it's easy to use twice as much as you need without realizing.

VINEGARS

Choose three or four vinegars—choose from red or white wine, cider, light malt, tarragon, sherry, or balsamic vinegar. Each will add its own character to your recipes.

MUSTARDS

Mustards are made from black, brown, or white mustard seeds which are ground, mixed with spices and then, usually, mixed with vinegar. Meaux mustard is made from mixed mustard seeds and has a grainy texture with a warm, spicy taste. Dijon mustard, made from husked and ground mustard seeds, is medium-hot and has a sharp flavor. Its versatility in salads and with barbecues makes it ideal for the vegetarian. German mustard is mild sweet/sour and is best used in Scandinavian and German dishes.

BOTTLED SAUCES

Soy sauce is widely used in Eastern cooking and is made from fermented yellow soybeans mixed with wheat, salt, yeast, and sugar. Light soy sauce tends to be rather salty, whereas dark soy sauce tends to be sweeter and is more often used in dips and sauces. Teriyaki sauce gives an authentic Japanese flavoring to stir-fries. Thick and dark brown, it contains soy sauce, vinegar, sesame oil, and spices as main ingredients. Black bean and yellow bean sauces add an instant authentic Chinese flavor to stir-fries. Black bean sauce is the stronger; the yellow bean variety is milder and is excellent with vegetables.

soups & appetizers

Soup is simple to make but always produces tasty results, and there is an enormous variety of vegetable soups. They can be rich and creamy, thick and chunky, light and delicate, and served hot or chilled. A wide range of ingredients can be used in addition to vegetables—beans, grains, noodles, cheese, and yogurt are all versatile ingredients.

Appetizers are an important part of any meal, setting the scene for the remainder of the menu and whetting the appetite. They should be colorful and full of flavor, but balance the remainder of the meal, not being too filling if a heavier main course is being served.

With this in mind, this chapter is packed with a variety of flavorful soups for all occasions and a wide range of appetizers from different origins. They will all make a wonderful snack or the first course of a meal.

mixed bean soup

serves 4

10 minutes

40 minutes

1 tbsp vegetable oil
1 red onion, halved and sliced
3 1/2 oz/100 g potato, diced
1 carrot, diced
1 leek, sliced
1 fresh green chile, sliced
3 garlic cloves, crushed
1 tsp ground coriander
1 tsp chili powder

4 cups vegetable stock
1 lb/450 g mixed canned beans, such as red kidney, cranberry, black-eye, or flageolet beans, drained
salt and pepper
2 tbsp chopped fresh cilantro, to garnish

This is a really hearty soup, filled with color, flavor, and goodness, which may be adapted to any vegetables that you have at hand.

cook's tip

Serve this soup with slices of warm corn bread or a cheese loaf.

Heat the oil in a large pan. Add the onion, potato, carrot, and leek and sauté for 2 minutes, stirring, until the vegetables are slightly softened.

Add the chile and crushed garlic and cook for an additional 1 minute.

Stir in the ground coriander, chili powder, and stock.

Bring the soup to a boil, then lower the heat and cook for 20 minutes, or until the vegetables are tender.

Stir in the beans, season well with salt and pepper, and cook for an additional 10 minutes, stirring occasionally.

Transfer the soup to a warmed tureen or individual serving bowls, garnish with chopped cilantro, and serve.

vegetable & corn
chowder

serves 4

15 minutes

30 minutes

1 tbsp vegetable oil
1 red onion, diced
1 red bell pepper, diced
3 garlic cloves, crushed
1 large potato, diced
2 tbsp all-purpose flour
2 1/2 cups milk
1 1/4 cups vegetable stock
1 3/4 oz/50 g broccoli florets

10 1/2 oz/300 g canned corn in brine, drained
scant 3/4 cup vegetarian Cheddar cheese, grated
salt and pepper
1 tbsp fresh cilantro leaves, to garnish

This is a really filling soup, which should be served before a lighter meal. Packed with corn and fresh vegetables it is easy to prepare and filled with flavor.

cook's tip

Add a little heavy cream to the soup after adding the milk for a really creamy flavor.

Vegetarian cheeses are made with rennets of nonanimal origin, using microbial or fungal enzymes.

Heat the oil in a large pan. Add the onion, bell pepper, garlic, and potato and sauté for 2–3 minutes, stirring.

Stir in the flour and cook for 30 seconds. Stir in the milk and stock.

Add the broccoli and corn. Bring the mixture to a boil, stirring, then lower the heat and let simmer for 20 minutes, or until the vegetables are tender.

Stir in scant 1/2 cup of the cheese until it melts.

Season to taste with salt and pepper, then spoon the chowder into a warmed soup tureen. Garnish with the remaining grated cheese and cilantro leaves and serve.

cauliflower & broccoli
soup with gruyère

 serves 4

 10 minutes

 35 minutes

3 tbsp vegetable oil
1 red onion, chopped
2 garlic cloves, crushed
10½ oz/300 g cauliflower florets
10½ oz/300 g broccoli florets
1 tbsp all-purpose flour
2½ cups milk
1¼ cups vegetable stock

scant ¾ cup vegetarian Gruyère cheese, grated
pinch of paprika, plus extra to garnish
⅔ cup light cream
vegetarian Gruyère cheese shavings, to garnish

This rich cauliflower and broccoli soup is very simple to make and delicious to eat.

cook's tip

The soup must not boil after the cream has been added, otherwise it will curdle. Use plain yogurt instead of the cream if preferred, but do not let boil.

Heat the oil in a large pan. Add the onion, garlic, cauliflower, and broccoli and sauté for 3–4 minutes, stirring constantly. Add the flour and cook for an additional 1 minute, stirring.

Stir in the milk and stock and bring to a boil. Lower the heat and let simmer for 20 minutes.

Remove one-quarter of the vegetables and set aside.

Place the remaining soup in a food processor or blender and process for 30 seconds, until smooth. Transfer the soup to a clean pan.

Return the reserved vegetable pieces to the soup.

Stir in the grated cheese, paprika, and light cream and heat gently for 2–3 minutes without boiling, or until the cheese starts to melt.

Transfer to warmed serving bowls, garnish with shavings of Gruyère cheese, and dust with paprika.

celery, stilton

& walnut soup

serves 4

10 minutes

30 minutes

scant 4 tbsp butter
2 shallots, chopped
3 celery stalks, chopped
1 garlic clove, crushed
2 tbsp all-purpose flour
2 1/2 cups vegetable stock
1 1/4 cups milk

5 1/2 oz/150 g blue Stilton cheese,
  crumbled, plus extra to garnish
2 tbsp walnut halves,
  coarsely chopped
2/3 cup plain yogurt
salt and pepper
celery leaves, to garnish

*This is a classic combination
of ingredients all brought
together in a delicious,
creamy soup.*

Melt the butter in a large pan. Add the shallots, celery, and garlic and sauté
for 2–3 minutes, stirring, until softened.

Add the flour and cook for 30 seconds.

Gradually stir in the stock and milk and bring to a boil.

Lower the heat to a gentle simmer and add the crumbled Stilton cheese
and walnut halves. Cover and let simmer for 20 minutes.

Stir in the yogurt and heat for an additional 2 minutes without boiling.

Season the soup with salt and pepper, then transfer to a warmed soup
tureen or individual serving bowls, garnish with celery leaves and extra
crumbled Stilton cheese, and serve at once.

cook's tip

*As well as adding protein, vitamins,
and useful fats to the diet, nuts add
important flavor and texture to
vegetarian meals.*

variation

*Use an alternative blue cheese,
such as Gorgonzola or a strong
vegetarian Cheddar cheese, grated,
if preferred.*

curried parsnip soup

serves 4

10 minutes

35 minutes

1 tbsp vegetable oil
1 tbsp butter
1 red onion, chopped
3 parsnips, chopped
2 garlic cloves, crushed
2 tsp garam masala
$\frac{1}{2}$ tsp chili powder

1 tbsp all-purpose flour
3$\frac{1}{2}$ cups vegetable stock
grated zest and juice of 1 lemon
salt and pepper
lemon zest, to garnish

Parsnips make a delicious soup as they have a slightly sweet flavor. In this recipe, spices are added to complement this sweetness and a dash of lemon juice adds tartness.

Heat the oil and butter in a large pan until the butter has melted.

Add the onion, parsnips, and garlic and sauté for 5–7 minutes, stirring, until the vegetables have softened.

Add the garam masala and chili powder and cook for 30 seconds, stirring.

Sprinkle in the flour, mixing well, and cook for an additional 30 seconds.

Stir in the stock, lemon zest and juice, and bring to a boil. Lower the heat and let simmer for 20 minutes.

Remove some of the vegetable pieces with a slotted spoon and set aside until required. Transfer the remaining soup and vegetables to a food processor or blender and process for 1 minute, or until smooth.

Return the soup to a clean pan and stir in the reserved vegetables. Reheat the soup gently for 2 minutes.

Season to taste with salt and pepper, then transfer to individual serving bowls, garnish with lemon zest, and serve at once.

variation

Use 1 medium orange instead of the lemon, if preferred, and garnish with grated orange zest.

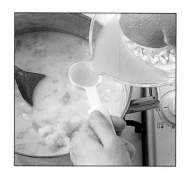

jerusalem artichoke soup

serves 4

10 minutes

30 minutes

1 lb 8 oz/675 g Jerusalem artichokes
5 tbsp orange juice
1 oz/25 g butter
1 leek, chopped
1 garlic clove, crushed
1 1/4 cups vegetable stock
2/3 cup milk

2 tbsp chopped fresh cilantro
2/3 cup plain yogurt
grated orange zest, to garnish

Jerusalem artichokes belong to the tuber family. They are native to North America, but are also grown in Europe. They have a delicious nutty flavor, which combines well with orange.

Wash the Jerusalem artichokes thoroughly in cold water and place in a large pan with 2 tablespoons of the orange juice and enough water to cover. Bring to a boil, then lower the heat and cook for 20 minutes, or until the artichokes are tender.

Drain the artichokes, reserving scant 2 cups of the cooking liquid. Let the artichokes cool.

Once cooled, peel the artichokes, and place in a large bowl. Mash the flesh with a potato masher.

Melt the butter in a large pan. Add the leek and garlic and sauté for 2–3 minutes, stirring, until the leek softens.

Stir in the artichoke flesh, the reserved cooking water, the stock, milk, and remaining orange juice. Bring the soup to a boil, lower the heat, and let simmer for 2–3 minutes.

Remove a few pieces of leek with a slotted spoon and set aside. Transfer the remainder of the soup to a food processor or blender and process for 1 minute, or until smooth.

Return the soup to a clean pan and stir in the reserved leeks, chopped cilantro, and yogurt.

Transfer to individual soup bowls, garnish with grated orange zest, and serve at once.

variation

If Jerusalem artichokes are unavailable, you could use sweet potatoes instead.

red bell pepper
& chile soup

serves 4

10 minutes

25 minutes

8 oz/225 g red bell peppers,
  seeded and sliced

1 onion, sliced

2 garlic cloves, crushed

1 fresh green chile, chopped

1 ¼ cups strained tomatoes

2 ½ cups vegetable stock

2 tbsp chopped fresh basil

fresh basil sprigs, to garnish

This soup has a real Mediterranean flavor, using sweet red bell peppers, tomato, chile, and basil. It is great served with warm olive bread.

Place the bell peppers in a large pan with the onion, garlic, and chile. Add the strained tomatoes and stock and bring to a boil, stirring well.

Lower the heat to a simmer and let simmer for 20 minutes, or until the bell peppers have softened. Drain, reserving the cooking liquid and vegetables separately.

Strain the vegetables by pressing through a strainer with the back of a spoon. Alternatively, transfer to a food processor and process briefly until smooth.

Return the vegetable purée to a clean pan with the reserved cooking liquid. Add the chopped basil and reheat gently until hot. Transfer to serving bowls, garnish with basil sprigs, and serve.

cook's tip

Basil is a useful herb to grow at home. It can be grown easily in a window box.

variation

This soup is also delicious served cold with ⅔ cup plain yogurt swirled into it.

dal soup

serves 4

5 minutes

40 minutes

2 tbsp butter
2 garlic cloves, crushed
1 onion, chopped
1/2 tsp ground turmeric
1 tsp garam masala
1/4 tsp chili powder
1 tsp ground cumin
2 lb 4 oz/1 kg canned chopped
   tomatoes, drained

1 cup split red lentils, rinsed
2 tsp lemon juice
2 1/2 cups vegetable stock
1 1/4 cups coconut milk
salt and pepper
warm naan bread, to serve

to garnish
chopped fresh cilantro
lemon slices

Dal is the name given to a delicious Indian lentil dish. This soup is a variation of the theme—it is made with split red lentils and spiced with curry powder.

cook's tip

You can buy canned coconut milk from supermarkets and delicatessens. It can also be made by grating creamed coconut, which comes in a solid bar, and mixing it with water.

Add small quantities of hot water to the pan while the lentils are cooking if they start to absorb too much of the liquid.

Melt the butter in a large pan. Add the garlic and onion and sauté for 2–3 minutes, stirring. Add the spices and cook for 30 seconds.

Stir in the tomatoes, lentils, lemon juice, stock, and coconut milk and bring to a boil.

Lower the heat and let simmer for 25–30 minutes, or until the lentils are cooked and tender.

Season to taste with salt and pepper, then ladle the soup into a warmed tureen or individual serving bowls. Garnish with chopped cilantro and lemon slices and serve with warm naan bread.

avocado & vegetable soup

serves 4

15 minutes

10 minutes

1 large ripe avocado
2 tbsp lemon juice
1 tbsp vegetable oil
1 3/4 oz/50 g canned corn, drained
2 tomatoes, peeled and seeded
1 garlic clove, crushed

1 leek, chopped
1 fresh red chile, chopped
scant 2 cups vegetable stock
2/3 cup milk
shredded leeks, to garnish

Avocado has a rich flavor and color, which makes a creamy flavored soup. It is best served chilled, but may be eaten warm as well.

cook's tip

To remove the pit from an avocado, first cut the avocado in half, then holding one half in your hand, rap the pit with a knife edge until it is embedded in the pit, then twist the knife until the pit is dislodged.

If serving chilled, transfer from the food processor to a bowl, stir in the stock and milk, cover, and let chill in the refrigerator for at least 4 hours.

Peel and mash the avocado with a fork, stir in the lemon juice, and set aside until required.

Heat the oil in a pan. Add the corn, tomatoes, garlic, leek, and chile and sauté for 2–3 minutes, or until the vegetables are softened.

Place half of the vegetable mixture in a food processor or blender with the avocado and process until smooth. Transfer to a clean pan.

Add the stock, milk, and reserved vegetables and cook gently for 3–4 minutes, until hot. Transfer to individual serving bowls, garnish with shredded leeks, and serve.

spanish tomato soup with garlic bread

serves 4

10 minutes

20 minutes

4 tbsp olive oil

1 onion, chopped

3 garlic cloves, crushed

1 green bell pepper, chopped

½ tsp chili powder

1 lb/450 g tomatoes, chopped

8 oz/225 g French or
   Italian bread, cubed

4 cups vegetable stock

garlic bread

4 slices ciabatta or French bread

4 tbsp olive oil

2 garlic cloves, crushed

¼ cup grated vegetarian Cheddar
   cheese

chili powder, to garnish

*This Mediterranean tomato soup
is thickened with bread, as is
traditional in some parts of Spain.*

Heat the oil in a large skillet. Add the onion, garlic, and bell pepper and sauté the vegetables for 2–3 minutes, or until the onion has softened.

Add the chili powder and tomatoes and cook over medium heat until the mixture has thickened.

Stir in the bread cubes and stock and cook for 10–15 minutes, until the soup is thick and fairly smooth.

variation

*Replace the green bell pepper with
red bell pepper, if you prefer.*

To make the garlic bread, preheat the broiler to medium. Toast the bread slices under the hot broiler. Drizzle the oil over the top of the bread, rub with the garlic, sprinkle with the cheese, and return to the broiler for 2–3 minutes, or until the cheese has melted. Sprinkle with chili powder and serve at once with the soup.

fava bean
& mint soup

serves 4

15 minutes

40 minutes

2 tbsp olive oil

1 red onion, chopped

2 garlic cloves, crushed

2 potatoes, diced

1 lb/450 g fava beans, thawed
    if frozen

3 1/2 cups vegetable stock

2 tbsp chopped fresh mint

to garnish

plain yogurt

fresh mint sprigs

*Fresh fava beans are best for this
recipe, but if they are unavailable,
use frozen beans instead.
They combine well with the
fresh flavor of mint.*

variation

*Use fresh cilantro and
1/2 teaspoon ground cumin as
flavorings in the soup, if you prefer.*

Heat the oil in a large pan. Add the onion and garlic and sauté for 2–3 minutes, until softened.

Add the potatoes and cook for 5 minutes, stirring well.

Stir in the beans and stock, cover, and let simmer for 30 minutes, or until the beans and potatoes are tender.

Remove a few vegetables with a slotted spoon and set aside until required. Place the remainder of the soup in a food processor or blender and process until smooth.

Return the soup to a clean pan and add the reserved vegetables and chopped mint. Stir well and reheat gently until hot.

Transfer the soup to a warmed tureen or individual serving bowls, garnish with swirls of yogurt and mint sprigs, and serve at once.

crispy potato skins

serves 4

30 minutes

1 hour 10 minutes

4 large baking potatoes
2 tbsp vegetable oil
4 tsp salt
fresh chives, to garnish
2/3 cup sour cream, to serve

bean sprout salad

scant 1/3 cup bean sprouts
1 celery stalk, sliced
1 orange, peeled and segmented
1 red eating apple, chopped
1/2 red bell pepper, chopped
1 tbsp chopped fresh parsley

1 tbsp light soy sauce
1 tbsp honey
1 small garlic clove, crushed

bean filling

3 1/2 oz/100 g canned
    mixed beans, drained
1 onion, halved and sliced
1 tomato, chopped
2 scallions, chopped
2 tsp lemon juice
salt and pepper

Potato skins are always a favorite. Prepare the skins in advance and warm through before serving with the salad fillings.

Preheat the oven to 400°F/200°C. Scrub the potatoes and place on a baking sheet. Prick the potatoes all over with a fork and rub the oil and salt into the skin.

Cook in the preheated oven for 1 hour, or until soft.

Using a sharp knife, cut the potatoes in half lengthwise and scoop out the flesh, leaving a 1/2-inch/1-cm thick shell. Place the shells, skin-side uppermost, in the hot oven for 10 minutes, until crisp.

Mix the ingredients for the bean sprout salad together in a bowl, tossing in the soy sauce, honey, and garlic to coat.

Mix all the ingredients together for the bean filling in a separate bowl.

Place the sour cream in a serving bowl and garnish with 2 tablespoons snipped chives.

Transfer the potato skins to serving plates, garnish with a few chive lengths, and serve hot with the salad fillings and sour cream.

tomato, olive & mozzarella bruschetta

serves 4

5–10 minutes

10 minutes

4 English muffins
4 garlic cloves, crushed
2 tbsp butter, softened
1 tbsp chopped fresh basil
4 large ripe tomatoes
1 tbsp tomato paste
8 pitted black olives, halved
1¾ oz/50 g mozzarella
   cheese, sliced

salt and pepper
fresh basil leaves, to garnish

dressing
1 tbsp olive oil
2 tsp lemon juice
1 tsp honey

These simple toasts are filled with color and flavor. They are great as a speedy appetizer or delicious with a good red wine.

Preheat the broiler to medium. Cut the English muffins in half to give 8 thick pieces. Toast the English muffin halves under the hot broiler for 2–3 minutes, until golden.

Mix the garlic, butter, and basil together in a bowl and spread onto each muffin half.

Cut a cross shape at the base of each tomato. Plunge the tomatoes in a bowl of boiling water—this will make the skin easier to peel. After a few minutes, pick each tomato up with a fork, and carefully peel away the skin. Chop the tomato flesh and mix with the tomato paste and olives. Divide the mixture between the English muffins.

variation

Use balsamic vinegar instead of the lemon juice for an authentic Mediterranean flavor.

Mix all the dressing ingredients together in a bowl and drizzle over each muffin. Arrange the mozzarella cheese on top and season to taste with salt and pepper.

Return the muffins to the broiler for 1–2 minutes, until the cheese melts.

Garnish with fresh basil leaves and serve at once.

lentil pâté

serves 4

30 minutes

1 hour 15 minutes

1 tbsp vegetable oil, plus extra
   for oiling
1 onion, chopped
2 garlic cloves, crushed
1 tsp garam masala
½ tsp ground coriander
3½ cups vegetable stock
1 cup split red lentils, rinsed
1 small egg

2 tbsp milk
2 tbsp mango chutney
2 tbsp chopped fresh parsley, plus
   extra to garnish

to serve

salad greens
warm toast

*Split red lentils are used in this
spicy recipe for speed as they
do not require presoaking. If you
have other lentils, soak and
precook them and use instead
of the split red lentils.*

variation

*Use other spices, such as chili
powder or Chinese five-spice
powder to flavor the pâté and
add tomato relish or chili relish
instead of the mango chutney,
if you prefer.*

Preheat the oven to 400°F/200°C. Oil and line the bottom of a 1-lb/450-g
loaf pan. Heat the oil in a large pan. Add the onion and garlic and sauté for
2–3 minutes, stirring. Add the spices and cook for 30 seconds.

Stir in the stock and lentils and bring the mixture to a boil. Lower the heat
and let simmer for 20 minutes, until the lentils are tender and cooked.
Remove the pan from the heat and drain off any excess moisture.

Place the mixture in a food processor and add the egg, milk, mango
chutney, and parsley. Process until smooth.

Spoon the mixture into the prepared pan, smoothing the surface. Cover
and cook in the preheated oven for 40–45 minutes, until firm to the touch.

Let the pâté cool in the pan for 20 minutes, then transfer to the
refrigerator to cool completely.

Turn out the pâté onto a serving plate, slice, and garnish with chopped
parsley. Serve with salad greens and warm toast.

roasted **vegetables**
on english **muffins**

serves 4

1 hour 15 minutes

30 minutes

1 red onion, cut into 8 pieces
1 eggplant, halved and sliced
1 yellow bell pepper, sliced
1 zucchini, sliced
4 tbsp olive oil
1 tbsp garlic vinegar
2 tbsp vermouth
2 garlic cloves, crushed
1 tbsp chopped fresh thyme
2 tsp light brown sugar
4 English muffins, halved

sauce

2 tbsp butter
1 tbsp flour
2/3 cup milk
1/3 cup vegetable stock
scant 3/4 cup vegetarian
  Cheddar cheese, grated
1 tsp whole-grain mustard
3 tbsp chopped fresh mixed herbs
salt and pepper

Roasted vegetables are delicious and attractive. Served on warm English muffins with a herb sauce, they are unbeatable.

Arrange the vegetables in a shallow ovenproof dish. Mix the oil, vinegar, vermouth, garlic, thyme, and sugar together in a measuring cup or pitcher and pour over the vegetables. Cover and let marinate for 1 hour.

Preheat the oven to 400°F/200°C. Transfer the vegetables to a baking sheet and cook in the preheated oven for 20–25 minutes, or until the vegetables have softened.

Meanwhile, make the sauce. Melt the butter in a small pan and add the flour. Cook for 1 minute, then remove the pan from the heat. Stir in the milk and stock and return the pan to the heat. Bring to a boil, stirring, until thickened. Stir in the cheese, mustard, and mixed herbs and season well with salt and pepper.

Preheat the broiler to high. Cut the English muffins in half and cook under the hot broiler for 2–3 minutes, or until golden brown, then remove and arrange on a serving plate.

Spoon the roasted vegetables onto the English muffins and pour the sauce over the top. Serve at once.

hummus & garlic toasts

serves 4

20 minutes

3 minutes

hummus

14 oz/400 g canned chickpeas
juice of 1 large lemon
6 tbsp sesame seed paste
2 tbsp olive oil
2 garlic cloves, crushed
salt and pepper

toasts

1 ciabatta loaf, sliced
2 garlic cloves, crushed
1 tbsp chopped fresh cilantro
4 tbsp olive oil

to garnish

chopped fresh cilantro
black olives

Hummus is a real favorite spread on these garlic toasts for a delicious appetizer or as part of a light lunch.

To make the hummus, drain the chickpeas, reserving a little of the liquid. Place the chickpeas and liquid in a food processor and process, gradually adding the reserved liquid and lemon juice. Process well after each addition until smooth.

Stir in the sesame seed paste and all but 1 teaspoon of the olive oil. Add the garlic, season to taste with salt and pepper, and process until smooth.

Spoon the hummus into a serving dish. Drizzle the remaining oil over the top and garnish with chopped cilantro and olives. Let chill in the refrigerator until required.

Preheat the broiler to medium. Arrange the slices of ciabatta on a broiler rack in a single layer.

Mix the garlic, cilantro, and oil together in a measuring cup or pitcher and drizzle over the bread slices. Cook under the hot broiler for 2–3 minutes, until golden brown, turning once. Serve hot with the hummus.

cook's tip

Make the hummus a day in advance and chill, covered, in the refrigerator until required. Garnish and serve.

mixed bean pâté

serves 4

45 minutes

–

14 oz/400 g canned mixed beans, drained

2 tbsp olive oil

juice of 1 lemon

2 garlic cloves, crushed

1 tbsp chopped fresh cilantro

2 scallions, chopped

salt and pepper

shredded scallion, to garnish

pita bread, to serve

This is a really quick appetizer to prepare if canned beans are used. Choose a wide variety of beans for color and flavor or use canned mixed beans.

cook's tip

Use canned beans which have no salt or sugar added and always rinse thoroughly before use.

Serve the pâté with warm pita bread or toast.

Rinse the beans thoroughly under cold running water and drain well.

Transfer the beans to a food processor or blender and process until smooth. Alternatively, place the beans in a bowl and mash with a fork or potato masher.

Add the oil, lemon juice, garlic, cilantro, and scallions and process until fairly smooth. Season to taste with salt and pepper.

Transfer the pâté to a serving bowl and let chill in the refrigerator for at least 30 minutes. Garnish with shredded scallions and serve with pita bread.

vegetable fritters with
sweet & sour sauce

serves 4

20 minutes

20 minutes

scant 1 cup whole-wheat flour
pinch of salt
pinch of cayenne pepper
4 tsp olive oil
$^3/_4$ cup cold water
$3^1/_2$ oz/100 g broccoli florets
$3^1/_2$ oz/100 g cauliflower florets
$1^3/_4$ oz/50 g snow peas
1 large carrot, cut into thin sticks
1 red bell pepper, sliced
2 egg whites, beaten
vegetable oil, for deep-frying

sauce
$^2/_3$ cup pineapple juice
$^2/_3$ cup vegetable stock
2 tbsp wine vinegar
2 tbsp light brown sugar
2 tsp cornstarch
2 scallions, chopped

These mixed vegetable fritters are coated in a light batter and deep-fried until golden for a deliciously crisp coating. They are ideal with the sweet-and-sour dipping sauce.

Sift the flour and salt into a large bowl and add the cayenne pepper. Make a well in the center and gradually beat in the oil and cold water to form a smooth batter.

Cook the vegetables in boiling water for 5 minutes and drain well.

Whisk the egg whites in a clean, dry bowl until peaks form, then fold into the flour batter.

Dip the vegetables into the batter, turning to coat well. Drain off any excess batter. Heat the oil for deep-frying in a deep-fryer or heavy-bottom pan to 350°F/180°C, or until a cube of bread browns in 30 seconds. Deep-fry the vegetables, in batches, for 1–2 minutes, until golden. Remove from the oil with a slotted spoon and drain on paper towels.

Place all the ingredients for the sauce in a pan and bring to a boil, stirring, until thickened and clear. Serve with the fritters.

mixed bhajis

serves 4

25 minutes

30 minutes

bhajis

generous 1 cup gram flour
1 tsp baking soda
salt and pepper
2 tsp ground coriander
1 tsp garam masala
1 1/2 tsp ground turmeric
1 1/2 tsp chili powder
2 tbsp chopped fresh cilantro
1 small onion, halved and sliced
1 small leek, sliced

3 1/2 oz/100 g cooked cauliflower
1/2–3/4 cup cold water
vegetable oil, for deep-frying

sauce

2/3 cup plain yogurt
2 tbsp chopped fresh mint
1/2 tsp ground turmeric
1 garlic clove, crushed
fresh mint sprigs, to garnish

These small bhajis are served in Indian restaurants as accompaniments to a main meal, but they are delicious as an appetizer with a small salad and yogurt sauce.

variation

If you prefer, use cooked broccoli instead of the cauliflower or cooked, drained spinach instead of the leek for a range of different flavored bhajis.

Sift the flour, baking soda, and salt to taste into a large bowl and add the spices and fresh cilantro. Mix well until thoroughly blended.

Divide the mixture into 3 portions and place in separate bowls. Stir the onion into one bowl, the leek into another, and the cauliflower into the third bowl. Add 3–4 tablespoons of water to each bowl and mix each to form a smooth paste.

Heat the oil for deep frying in a deep-fryer or heavy-bottom pan to 350°F/180°C, or until a cube of bread browns in 30 seconds. Using 2 dessert spoons, form the mixture into circles and deep-fry each circle in the hot oil for 3–4 minutes, until browned. Remove with a slotted spoon and drain on paper towels. Keep the bhajis warm in the oven while cooking the remainder.

Mix all the sauce ingredients together in a measuring cup or pitcher and pour into a serving bowl. Garnish with mint sprigs and serve with the warm bhajis.

mushroom & garlic soufflés

 serves 4

 10 minutes

 20 minutes

1¾ oz/50 g butter, plus extra
   for greasing
2¾ oz/75 g flat mushrooms, chopped
2 tsp lime juice
2 garlic cloves, crushed
2 tbsp chopped fresh marjoram

2 tbsp all-purpose flour
1 cup milk
salt and pepper
2 eggs, separated

These individual soufflés are very impressive appetizers, but must be cooked just before serving to prevent them sinking.

cook's tip

Insert a skewer into the center of the soufflés to test if they are cooked through—it should come out clean. If not, cook for a few minutes longer, but do not overcook, otherwise they will become rubbery.

Preheat the oven to 400°F/200°C. Lightly grease the inside of 4 x ⅔-cup individual soufflé dishes with a little butter.

Melt 2 tablespoons of the butter in a skillet. Add the mushrooms, lime juice, and garlic and sauté for 2–3 minutes. Remove the mushroom mixture from the skillet with a slotted spoon and transfer to a large bowl. Stir in the marjoram.

Melt the remaining butter in a pan. Add the flour and cook for 1 minute, then remove the pan from the heat. Stir in the milk and return to the heat. Bring to a boil, stirring, until thickened. Season to taste with salt and pepper.

Add the sauce to the mushroom mixture, mixing well, then beat in the egg yolks.

Whisk the egg whites in a clean, dry bowl until peaks form, then fold into the mushroom mixture until fully incorporated.

Divide the mixture between the soufflé dishes. Place the dishes on a baking sheet and cook in the preheated oven for 8–10 minutes, or until the soufflés have risen and are cooked through. Serve at once.

carrot, fennel &
potato medley

serves 4

5 minutes

5 minutes

2 tbsp olive oil
1 potato, cut into thin strips
1 fennel bulb, cut into thin strips
2 carrots, grated
1 red onion, cut into thin strips

dressing
3 tbsp olive oil
1 tbsp garlic wine vinegar

1 garlic clove, crushed
1 tsp Dijon mustard
2 tsp honey
salt and pepper

to garnish
chopped fresh chives
fennel fronds

This is a colorful dish of shredded vegetables in a fresh garlic and honey dressing. It is delicious served with crusty bread to mop up the dressing.

Heat the olive oil in a skillet. Add the potato and fennel slices and cook for 2–3 minutes, until starting to brown. Remove from the skillet with a slotted spoon and drain on paper towels.

Arrange the carrot, red onion, potato, and fennel in separate piles on a serving platter.

Mix all the dressing ingredients together in a bowl and pour over the vegetables. Toss well and sprinkle with chopped chives and fennel fronds. Serve at once or let chill in the refrigerator until required.

cook's tip

Fennel is an aromatic plant which has a delicate, anise flavor. It can be eaten raw in salads, or boiled, braised, sautéed, or broiled. For this salad, if fennel is unavailable, substitute 12 oz/350 g sliced leeks.

variation

Use mixed, broiled bell peppers or shredded leeks in this dish for variety, or add bean sprouts and a segmented orange, if you prefer.

onions à la grecque

serves 4

10 minutes

15 minutes

1 lb/450 g shallots
3 tbsp olive oil
3 tbsp honey
2 tbsp garlic wine vinegar
3 tbsp dry white wine

1 tbsp tomato paste
2 celery stalks, sliced
2 tomatoes, seeded and chopped
salt and pepper
chopped celery leaves,
   to garnish

This is a well-known method of cooking vegetables and is perfect with shallots or onions, served with a crisp salad.

Peel the shallots. Heat the oil in a large pan. Add the shallots and cook, stirring, for 3–5 minutes, or until they start to brown.

Add the honey and cook for an additional 30 seconds over high heat, then add the vinegar and white wine, stirring well.

Stir in the tomato paste, celery, and tomatoes and bring the mixture to a boil. Cook over high heat for 5–6 minutes. Season to taste with salt and pepper and let cool slightly.

Garnish with chopped celery leaves and serve warm or cold.

cook's tip

This dish, served warm, would also make an ideal accompaniment to Chickpea Roast (page 115).

variation

Use white mushrooms instead of the shallots, and fennel instead of the celery for another appetizer.

eggplant timbale

serves 4

30 minutes

45 minutes

1 large eggplant
butter, for greasing
1¾ oz/50 g dried macaroni
1 tbsp vegetable oil
1 onion, chopped
2 garlic cloves, crushed
2 tbsp drained canned corn
2 tbsp frozen peas, thawed
generous 2 cups fresh spinach leaves
¼ cup vegetarian Cheddar cheese, grated

1 egg, beaten
8 oz/225 g canned chopped tomatoes
1 tbsp chopped fresh basil
salt and pepper

sauce
4 tbsp olive oil
2 tbsp white wine vinegar
2 garlic cloves, crushed
3 tbsp chopped fresh basil
1 tbsp superfine sugar

This is a great way to serve pasta as an appetizer, wrapped in an eggplant mold. It looks really impressive yet it is so easy to make.

Preheat the oven to 350°F/180°C. Using a potato peeler, cut the eggplant lengthwise into thin strips Place in a bowl of boiling salted water and let stand for 3–4 minutes. Drain the eggplant strips well.

Grease 4 x ⅔-cup individual ramekins and use the eggplant strips to line the dishes, leaving 1 inch/2.5 cm of eggplant overlapping.

Cook the pasta in a large pan of boiling water for 8–10 minutes, or until tender but still firm to the bite. Drain. Heat the oil in a separate pan. Add the onion and garlic and sauté for 2–3 minutes. Stir in the corn and peas, then remove the pan from the heat.

Blanch the spinach, drain well, chop, and set aside. Add the pasta to the onion mixture with the cheese, egg, tomatoes, and basil. Season with salt and pepper and mix. Half-fill each ramekin with some of the pasta. Place the spinach on top and then the remaining pasta mixture. Fold the eggplant over the filling to cover. Place the ramekins in a roasting pan half-filled with boiling water, then cover and cook in the preheated oven for 20–25 minutes, or until set. Meanwhile, heat all the ingredients for the sauce in a pan. Turn out the ramekins and serve with the sauce.

snacks &
light meals

The ability to rustle up a simple snack or a quickly prepared light meal can be very important in our busy lives. Sometimes we may not feel like eating a full-scale meal but nevertheless want something appetizing and satisfying. Whether it is for a sustaining snack to break the day, hearty nibbles to serve with pre-dinner drinks, or an informal lunch or supper party, you will find a mouthwatering collection of recipes in this chapter. They cater for all tastes and times of day, and many can be prepared ahead of time and will not detain you in the kitchen for too long.

There are many easy-to-prepare dishes in this chapter which will satisfy your hunger as well as your taste buds. You will easily find something to sustain you, which is lighter than main meal dishes, but which may also be served with an accompaniment or crisp salad.

garlic mushrooms on toast

serves 4

10 minutes

10 minutes

2³/4 oz/75 g vegetarian margarine
2 garlic cloves, crushed
12 oz/350 g mixed mushrooms, such as open-cap, white, oyster, and shiitake, sliced

8 slices French bread
1 tbsp chopped fresh parsley
salt and pepper

This is so simple to prepare and looks great if you use a variety of mushrooms for shape and texture. Cooked in garlic butter, they are simply irresistible.

Preheat the broiler to medium. Melt the margarine in a skillet. Add the crushed garlic and cook for 30 seconds, stirring.

Add the mushrooms and cook for 5 minutes, turning occasionally.

Toast the slices of French bread under the hot broiler for 2–3 minutes, turning once. Transfer the toasts to a serving plate.

Toss the chopped parsley into the mushrooms, mixing thoroughly, then season well with salt and pepper.

Spoon the mushroom mixture over the toasts and serve at once.

cook's tip

Add seasonings, such as curry powder or chili powder, to the mushrooms for extra flavor, if liked.

Store mushrooms for 24–36 hours in the refrigerator, in paper bags, as they sweat in plastic. Exotic mushrooms should be washed, but other varieties can simply be wiped with paper towels.

potato, bell pepper & mushroom hash

serves 4

15 minutes

30 minutes

1 lb 8 oz/675 g potatoes, cubed
salt and pepper
1 tbsp olive oil
2 garlic cloves, crushed
1 green bell pepper, cubed
1 yellow bell pepper, cubed
3 tomatoes, diced

2¾ oz/75 g white mushrooms, halved
1 tbsp vegetarian Worcestershire sauce
2 tbsp chopped fresh basil
fresh basil sprigs, to garnish
warmed crusty bread, to serve

This is a quick one-pan dish, which is ideal for a quick snack. Packed with color and flavor it is very versatile and you can add any other vegetable you have at hand.

Cook the potatoes in a pan of boiling salted water for 7–8 minutes. Drain well and set aside.

Heat the oil in a large, heavy-bottom skillet. Add the potatoes and cook for 8–10 minutes, stirring, until browned.

Add the garlic and bell peppers and cook for 2–3 minutes.

Stir in the tomatoes and mushrooms and cook, stirring, for 5–6 minutes.

Stir in the Worcestershire sauce and chopped basil and season well with salt and pepper. Garnish with basil sprigs and serve with crusty bread.

cook's tip

Most brands of Worcestershire sauce contain anchovies so choose a vegetarian variety.

variation

This dish can also be eaten cold as a salad.

vegetable **samosas**

makes 12

20 minutes

30 minutes

2 tbsp vegetable oil, plus extra for deep-frying
1 onion, chopped
1/2 tsp ground coriander
1/2 tsp ground cumin
pinch of ground turmeric
1/2 tsp ground ginger
1/2 tsp garam masala
1 garlic clove, crushed

8 oz/225 g potatoes, diced
scant 1 cup frozen peas, thawed
scant 3 1/2 cups fresh spinach, chopped
12 sheets phyllo pastry
lemon slices, to garnish

These Indian snacks are perfect for a quick or light meal. Served with a salad they can be made in advance and frozen for ease.

Heat the 2 tablespoons of oil in a skillet. Add the onion and sauté for 1–2 minutes, stirring, until softened. Stir in all the spices and garlic and cook for 1 minute.

Add the potatoes and cook over low heat for 5 minutes, stirring, until they start to soften.

Stir in the peas and spinach and cook for an additional 3–4 minutes.

Lay the phyllo pastry sheets out on a clean counter and fold each sheet in half lengthwise.

Place 2 tablespoons of the vegetable filling at one end of each folded pastry sheet. Fold over one corner to make a triangle. Continue folding in this way to make a triangular package and seal the edges with water.

Repeat with the remaining pastry and filling.

cook's tip

Serve with a yogurt sauce (see Cook's Tip on page 101) and a salad.

Heat the oil for deep-frying in a heavy-bottom pan to 350°F/180°C, or until a cube of bread browns in 30 seconds. Deep-fry the samosas, in batches, for 1–2 minutes, until golden. Drain on paper towels and keep warm while cooking the remainder. Transfer the samosas to a serving plate, garnish with lemon slices, and serve.

scrambled tofu on toast

serves 4

5–10 minutes

5 minutes

2³⁄4 oz/75 g vegetarian margarine
1 lb/450 g smoked firm tofu
   (drained weight)
1 red onion, chopped
1 red bell pepper, chopped
4 ciabatta rolls

2 tbsp chopped fresh mixed herbs
salt and pepper
fresh herbs, to garnish

This is a delicious dish, which would also serve as a light lunch or supper.

Preheat the broiler to medium. Melt the margarine in a large skillet.

Crumble the tofu into the skillet, then add the onion and bell pepper and cook for 3–4 minutes, stirring occasionally.

Meanwhile, slice the ciabatta rolls in half and toast under the hot broiler for 2–3 minutes, turning once. Remove the toasts and transfer to a large serving plate.

Add the herbs to the tofu mixture and mix well. Season to taste with salt and pepper.

Spoon the tofu mixture onto the toast and garnish with fresh herbs. Serve at once.

cook's tip

Smoked tofu adds extra flavor to this dish. Marinated tofu could be used instead.

Rub the cut surface of a garlic clove over the toasted ciabatta rolls for extra flavor.

mixed bean pan-fry

serves 4

10 minutes

15 minutes

12 oz/350 g mixed green beans, such as string and fava beans
2 tbsp vegetable oil
2 garlic cloves, crushed
1 red onion, halved and sliced
8 oz/225 g firm marinated tofu, diced
1 tbsp lemon juice

¾ tsp ground turmeric
1 tsp ground allspice
⅔ cup vegetable stock
2 tsp sesame seeds

Fresh green beans have a wonderful flavor that is hard to beat. If you cannot find fresh beans, use thawed, frozen beans instead.

Trim and slice the string beans, then shell the fava beans and set aside until required.

Heat the oil in a large skillet. Add the garlic and onion and sauté for 2 minutes, stirring well.

Add the tofu and cook for 2–3 minutes, until just starting to brown.

Add the reserved string beans and fava beans. Stir in the lemon juice, turmeric, allspice, and stock and bring to a boil.

Lower the heat and let simmer for 5–7 minutes, or until the beans are tender. Sprinkle with sesame seeds and serve at once.

variation

Add lime juice instead of lemon, for an alternative citrus flavor.

Use smoked tofu instead of marinated tofu, if you prefer.

calzone with sun-dried tomatoes & vegetables

serves 4

1 hour 30 minutes

40 minutes

dough

3 cups strong white flour, plus extra for dusting

2 tsp active dry yeast

1 tsp superfine sugar

$^2\!/_3$ cup vegetable stock

$^2\!/_3$ cup strained tomatoes

vegetable oil, for oiling

1 egg, beaten

filling

1 tbsp vegetable oil

1 onion, chopped

1 garlic clove, crushed

2 tbsp chopped sun-dried tomatoes

generous 2 cups fresh spinach, chopped

3 tbsp canned drained corn

1 oz/25 g green beans, cut into 3 pieces

1 tbsp tomato paste

1 tbsp chopped fresh oregano

salt and pepper

1$^3\!/_4$ oz/50 g mozzarella cheese, sliced

These pizza base packages are great for making in advance and freezing—they can be thawed when required for a quick snack.

Sift the flour into a bowl. Add the yeast and sugar and beat in the stock and strained tomatoes to form a smooth dough.

Knead the dough on a lightly floured counter for 10 minutes, then place in a clean, lightly oiled bowl and let rise in a warm place for 1 hour.

Preheat the oven to 425°F/220°C. To make the filling, heat the oil in a large skillet. Add the onion and sauté for 2–3 minutes. Stir in the garlic, tomatoes, spinach, corn, and beans and cook for 3–4 minutes. Add the tomato paste and oregano and season well with salt and pepper.

Divide the risen dough into 4 equal-size portions and roll each onto a floured counter to form a 7-inch/18-cm circle. Spoon a quarter of the filling onto one half of each circle and top with the cheese. Fold the dough over to encase the filling, sealing the edge with a fork. Glaze with beaten egg. Place the calzone on an oiled baking sheet and cook in the preheated oven for 25–30 minutes, or until risen and golden. Serve warm.

vegetable enchiladas

serves 4

20 minutes

55 minutes

4 flour tortillas

scant ¾ cup vegetarian Cheddar cheese, grated

filling

scant 1¾ cups fresh spinach leaves

2 tbsp olive oil

8 baby corn, sliced

¼ cup frozen peas, thawed

1 red bell pepper, diced

1 carrot, diced

1 leek, sliced

2 garlic cloves, crushed

1 fresh red chile, chopped

salt and pepper

sauce

1¼ cups strained tomatoes

2 shallots, chopped

1 garlic clove, crushed

1¼ cups vegetable stock

1 tsp superfine sugar

1 tsp chili powder

This Mexican dish uses prepared tortillas, which are readily available in supermarkets. They are filled with a spicy vegetable mixture and topped with a hot tomato sauce.

Preheat the oven to 350°F/180°C. To make the filling, blanch the spinach in a pan of boiling water for 2 minutes, drain well, and chop. Set aside until required.

Heat the oil in a large skillet. Add the corn, peas, bell pepper, carrot, leek, garlic, and chile and sauté for 3–4 minutes, stirring briskly. Stir in the spinach and season well with salt and pepper.

Place all the sauce ingredients in a pan and bring to a boil, stirring. Cook over high heat for 20 minutes, stirring constantly, until thickened and reduced by one-third.

Spoon one-quarter of the filling along the center of each tortilla. Roll the tortillas round the filling and place in an ovenproof dish, seam-side down.

Pour the sauce over the tortillas and sprinkle the cheese on top. Cook in the preheated oven for 20 minutes, or until the cheese has melted and browned. Serve at once.

spinach gnocchi with
tomato & basil sauce

serves 4

25 minutes

1 hour

1 lb/450 g baking potatoes
salt and pepper
scant 1¾ cups fresh spinach leaves
1 tsp water
2 tbsp butter or vegetarian
    margarine
1 small egg, beaten
generous 1 cup all-purpose flour, plus
    extra for dusting
fresh basil sprigs, to garnish

tomato sauce
1 tbsp olive oil
1 shallot, chopped
1 tbsp tomato paste
8 oz/225 g canned chopped tomatoes
2 tbsp chopped fresh basil
⅓ cup red wine
1 tsp superfine sugar

These gnocchi or small dumplings are made with potato and flavored with spinach and nutmeg, then served in a rich tomato sauce for an ideal light meal.

Cook the potatoes in their skins in a pan of boiling salted water for 20 minutes. Drain well and press through a strainer into a bowl. Cook the spinach in the water for 5 minutes, until wilted. Drain and pat dry with paper towels. Chop and stir into the potatoes.

Add the butter, egg, and half of the flour to the spinach mixture, mixing well. Turn out onto a floured counter, gradually kneading in the remaining flour to form a soft dough. With floured hands, roll the dough into thin ropes and cut off ¾-inch/2-cm pieces. Press the center of each dumpling with your finger, drawing it toward you to curl the sides of the gnocchi. Cover and let chill in the refrigerator.

Heat the oil for the sauce in a pan. Add the chopped shallot and sauté for 5 minutes. Add the tomato paste, tomatoes, basil, red wine, and sugar and season well with salt and pepper. Bring to a boil, then let simmer for 20 minutes.

Bring a large pan of lightly salted water to a boil. Add the gnocchi and cook for 2–3 minutes, or until they rise to the top of the pan. Drain well and transfer to serving dishes. Spoon the tomato sauce over the top. Garnish with basil sprigs and serve.

vegetable **jambalaya**

serves 4

 10 minutes

 55 minutes

generous ⅜ cup brown rice
2 tbsp olive oil
2 garlic cloves, crushed
1 red onion, cut into 8 wedges
1 eggplant, diced
1 green bell pepper, diced
1¾ oz/50 g baby corn,
   halved lengthwise
generous ⅜ cup frozen peas

3½ oz/100 g small broccoli florets
⅔ cup vegetable stock
8 oz/225 g canned chopped tomatoes
1 tbsp tomato paste
1 tsp creole seasoning
½ tsp red pepper flakes
salt and pepper

*This dish traditionally contains
spicy sausage, but it is equally
delicious filled with vegetables in
this spicy vegetarian version.*

cook's tip

*Use a mixture of rice,
such as wild or red rice, for color
and texture. Cook the rice in
advance for a speedier recipe.*

Cook the rice in a large pan of boiling water for 20 minutes, or until cooked through. Drain and set aside until required.

Heat the oil in a heavy-bottom skillet. Add the garlic and onion and cook for 2–3 minutes, stirring.

Add the eggplant, bell pepper, corn, peas, and broccoli to the skillet and cook, stirring occasionally, for 2–3 minutes.

Stir in the stock, canned tomatoes, tomato paste, creole seasoning, and red pepper flakes. Season to taste with salt and pepper and cook over low heat for 15–20 minutes, or until the vegetables are tender.

Stir the brown rice into the vegetable mixture and cook, mixing well, for 3–4 minutes, or until hot. Transfer the vegetable jambalaya to warmed serving dishes and serve at once.

stuffed mushrooms

serves 4

15 minutes

25 minutes

8 open-cap mushrooms

1 tbsp olive oil

1 small leek, chopped

1 celery stalk, chopped

3 1/2 oz/100 g firm tofu, diced (drained weight)

1 zucchini, chopped

1 carrot, chopped

1 3/4 cups fresh whole-wheat bread crumbs

2 tbsp chopped fresh basil

1 tbsp tomato paste

2 tbsp pine nuts

scant 3/4 cup vegetarian Cheddar cheese, grated

2/3 cup vegetable stock

salt and pepper

Use large open-cap mushrooms for this recipe for their flavor and suitability for filling.

cook's tip

Vary the vegetables used for flavor and color or according to those you have available.

Preheat the oven to 425°F/220°C. Remove the stalks from the mushrooms and chop finely.

Heat the oil in a large skillet. Add the chopped mushroom stalks, leek, celery, tofu, zucchini, and carrot and cook for 3–4 minutes, stirring.

Stir in the bread crumbs, basil, tomato paste, and pine nuts. Season to taste with salt and pepper.

Spoon the mixture into the mushrooms and top with the cheese.

Place the mushrooms in a shallow ovenproof dish and pour the vegetable stock round them.

Cook in the preheated oven for 20 minutes, or until cooked through and the cheese has melted. Remove the mushrooms from the dish and serve.

vegetable crêpes

serves 4

15 minutes

45 minutes

crêpes
²/₃ cup all-purpose flour
pinch of salt
1 egg, beaten
1¹/₄ cups milk
vegetable oil, for cooking

filling
2 tbsp vegetable oil
1 leek, shredded
¹/₂ tsp chili powder
¹/₂ tsp ground cumin
1³/₄ oz/50 g snow peas
3¹/₂ oz/100 g white mushrooms

1 red bell pepper, sliced
2 tbsp cashews, chopped

sauce
2 tbsp vegetarian margarine
2 tbsp all-purpose flour
²/₃ cup vegetable stock
²/₃ cup milk
1 tsp Dijon mustard
scant ³/₄ cup vegetarian Cheddar
    cheese, grated
2 tbsp chopped fresh cilantro

*Crêpes are ideal for filling with
your favorite ingredients. In this
recipe they are packed with
a spicy vegetable filling, which
may be made in advance and
reheated for serving.*

To make the crêpes, sift the flour and salt into a large bowl. Beat in the egg and milk to form a batter. For the filling, heat the oil in a skillet. Add the leek and sauté for 2–3 minutes. Add the remaining ingredients and cook for 5 minutes, stirring.

To make the sauce, melt the margarine in a pan. Add the flour and cook for 1 minute, then remove the pan from the heat. Stir in the stock and milk and return the pan to the heat. Bring to a boil, stirring, until thick. Add the mustard, half of the cheese, and the cilantro and cook for 1 minute.

Preheat the broiler to medium. Heat 1 tablespoons of oil for cooking in a nonstick 6-inch/15-cm skillet. Pour the oil from the skillet and add an eighth of the batter to cover the bottom of the skillet. Cook for 2 minutes, then turn the crêpe over and cook the other side for 1 minute. Repeat with the remaining batter.

Spoon a little of the filling along the center of each crêpe and roll up. Place in a heatproof dish and pour the sauce on top. Top with the remaining cheese and heat under the hot broiler for 3–5 minutes, or until the cheese melts and turns golden. Transfer to serving plates and serve.

vegetable pasta nests

serves 4

25 minutes

40 minutes

6 oz/175 g dried spaghetti
1 eggplant, halved and sliced
1 zucchini, diced
1 red bell pepper, seeded and diagonally chopped
6 tbsp olive oil
2 garlic cloves, crushed

1³/4 oz/50 g butter or vegetarian margarine, melted
1/8 cup dry white bread crumbs
salt and pepper
fresh parsley sprigs, to garnish

These large pasta nests look impressive when presented filled with broiled mixed vegetables, and taste delicious.

Preheat the broiler to high and the oven to 400°F/200°C. Bring a large pan of water to a boil. Add the pasta, return to a boil, and cook for 10–12 minutes, or until "al dente." Drain well and set aside.

Place the eggplant, zucchini, and bell pepper on a baking sheet.

Mix the oil and garlic together in a small measuring cup and pour over the vegetables, tossing to coat.

Cook under the hot broiler for 10 minutes, turning, until tender and lightly charred. Set aside and keep warm.

Divide the spaghetti between 4 lightly greased Yorkshire pudding pans or muffin pans. Using a fork, curl the spaghetti to form nests.

cook's tip

"Al dente" means "to the bite" and describes cooked pasta that is not too soft, but still has a bite to it.

Brush the pasta nests with melted butter and sprinkle with the bread crumbs. Bake in the preheated oven for 15 minutes, or until lightly golden. Remove the pasta nests from the pans and transfer to serving plates. Divide the broiled vegetables between the pasta nests, season to taste with salt and pepper, and garnish with parsley. Serve.

burgers & fries

serves 4

45 minutes

1 hour

burgers

generous 2 cups fresh spinach leaves

1 tbsp olive oil

1 leek, chopped

2 garlic cloves, crushed

3 1/2 oz/100 g mushrooms, chopped

10 1/2 oz/300 g firm tofu, chopped (drained weight)

1 tsp chili powder

1 tsp curry powder

1 tbsp chopped fresh cilantro

1 3/8 cups fresh whole-wheat bread crumbs

all-purpose flour, for dusting

1 tbsp olive oil, for cooking

french fries

2 large potatoes

2 tbsp flour

1 tsp chili powder

2 tbsp olive oil

to serve

burger bap or roll

crisp salad

These spicy vegetable burgers are delicious, especially when served with the light oven fries. Serve them in a warm bun or roll with radicchio lettuce leaves and red onion relish.

To make the burgers, cook the spinach in a little water for 2 minutes. Drain thoroughly and pat dry with paper towels.

Heat the oil in a large skillet. Add the leek and garlic and sauté for 2–3 minutes. Add the remaining ingredients except for the bread crumbs and cook for 5–7 minutes, until the vegetables have softened. Toss in the spinach and cook for 1 minute.

Transfer the mixture to a food processor and process for 30 seconds, or until almost smooth. Stir in the bread crumbs, mixing well, and let stand until cool enough to handle. Using lightly floured hands, form the mixture into 4 equal-size burgers. Let chill in the refrigerator for 30 minutes.

Preheat the oven to 400°F/200°C. To make the french fries, cut the potatoes into thin wedges and cook in a pan of boiling water for 10 minutes. Drain and toss in the flour and chili. Lay the french fries on a baking sheet and sprinkle with the oil. Cook in the preheated oven for 30 minutes, or until golden.

Meanwhile, heat the oil for cooking in a skillet. Add the burgers and cook for 8–10 minutes, turning once. Serve in a bap with salad and french fries.

vegetable dim sum

serves 4

15 minutes

15 minutes

2 scallions, chopped
1 oz/25 g green beans, chopped
½ small carrot, finely chopped
1 fresh red chile, chopped
2 tbsp bean sprouts, chopped
1 oz/25 g white mushrooms, chopped
2 tbsp unsalted cashews, chopped
1 small egg, beaten

2 tbsp cornstarch
1 tsp light soy sauce
1 tsp hoisin sauce
1 tsp sesame oil
32 won ton skins
vegetable oil, for deep-frying
1 tbsp sesame seeds

Dim sum are small Chinese packages, usually served as part of a large mixed meal. They may be filled with any variety of fillings, steamed, or cooked and served with a dipping sauce.

cook's tip

If preferred, arrange the won tons on a heatproof plate and steam in a steamer for 5–7 minutes for a healthier cooking method.

Mix all of the vegetables together in a bowl.

Add the nuts, egg, cornstarch, soy sauce, hoisin sauce, and sesame oil to the bowl, stirring to mix well.

Lay the won ton skins out on a cutting board and spoon small quantities of the mixture into the center of each. Gather the skin round the filling at the top to make little packages, leaving the top open.

Heat the oil for deep-frying in a wok or heavy-bottom pan to 350°F/180°C, or until a cube of bread browns in 30 seconds.

Deep-fry the won tons, in batches, for 1–2 minutes, or until golden. Drain on paper towels and keep warm while cooking the remaining won tons.

Sprinkle the sesame seeds over the won tons and serve.

cheese & garlic
mushroom pizzas

serves 4

45 minutes

30 minutes

dough

3 cups strong white flour, plus extra for dusting

2 tsp active dry yeast

2 garlic cloves, crushed

2 tbsp chopped fresh thyme

2 tbsp olive oil

1 1/4 cups tepid water

butter, for greasing

topping

2 tbsp butter or margarine

12 oz/350 g mixed mushrooms, sliced

2 garlic cloves, crushed

2 tbsp chopped fresh parsley

2 tbsp tomato paste

6 tbsp strained tomatoes

scant 3/4 cup mozzarella cheese, grated

salt and pepper

chopped fresh parsley, to garnish

This pizza dough is flavored with garlic and herbs and topped with mixed mushrooms and melting cheese for a really delicious pizza.

Place the flour, yeast, garlic, and thyme in a bowl. Make a well in the center and gradually stir in the oil and water. Bring together to form a soft dough.

Turn the dough onto a floured counter and knead for 5 minutes, or until smooth. Roll into a 14-inch/35-cm circle and place on a greased baking sheet. Leave in a warm place for 20 minutes, or until the dough puffs up.

Meanwhile, preheat the oven to 375°F/190°C. To make the topping, melt the butter in a skillet. Add the mushrooms, garlic, and parsley and sauté for 5 minutes.

cook's tip

If preferred, spread the base with a prepared cheese sauce before adding the mushrooms.

Mix the tomato paste and strained tomatoes together and spoon onto the pizza base, leaving a 1/2-inch/1-cm edge of dough. Spoon the mushroom mixture on top. Season with salt and pepper and sprinkle the cheese on top. Cook the pizza in the preheated oven for 20–25 minutes, or until the base is crisp and the cheese has melted. Garnish with parsley and serve.

watercress & cheese tartlets

serves 4

20 minutes

25 minutes

2/3 cup all-purpose flour, plus extra
   for dusting
pinch of salt
2¾ oz/75 g butter or vegetarian
   margarine
2–3 tbsp cold water
2 bunches of watercress

2 garlic cloves, crushed
1 shallot, chopped
1³/8 cups vegetarian Cheddar cheese,
   grated
2 tbsp plain yogurt
½ tsp paprika

*These individual tartlets
are great for lunchtime or for
picnic food. Watercress is a good
source of folic acid, which is
important in early pregnancy.*

cook's tip

*Use spinach instead of the
watercress, making sure it is well
drained before mixing with the
remaining filling ingredients.*

Preheat the oven to 350°F/180°C. Sift the flour into a large bowl and add
the salt. Rub 1¾ oz/50 g of the butter into the flour until the mixture
resembles bread crumbs.

Stir in the cold water to form a dough.

Roll the dough out on a lightly floured counter and use to line
4 x 4-inch/10-cm tartlet pans. Prick the bases with a fork and let chill
until required.

Heat the remaining butter in a large skillet. Discard the stems from the
watercress and add to the skillet with the garlic and shallot, cooking for
1–2 minutes, until the watercress is wilted.

Remove the skillet from the heat and stir in the grated cheese, plain
yogurt, and paprika.

Spoon the mixture into the pastry shells and cook in the preheated oven
for 20 minutes, or until the filling is firm. Turn out the tartlets and serve.

vegetable-filled ravioli

serves 4

20 minutes

20 minutes

filling
2 tbsp butter or
   vegetarian margarine
2 garlic cloves, crushed
1 small leek, chopped
2 celery stalks, chopped
7 oz/200 g open-cap mushrooms,
   chopped
1 egg, beaten

2 tbsp freshly grated vegetarian
   Parmesan cheese
salt and pepper

ravioli
4 sheets phyllo pastry
2 tbsp butter or vegetarian
   margarine, melted
vegetable oil, for deep-frying

These small packages are very easy to make and have the advantage of being filled with your favorite mixture of succulent mushrooms. Serve with freshly grated cheese sprinkled on top.

cook's tip

Parmesan cheese is generally nonvegetarian, however, there is an Italian Parmesan called Grano Padano, which is usually vegetarian. Alternatively, you could use romano cheese.

To make the filling, melt the butter in a skillet. Add the garlic and leek and sauté for 2–3 minutes, until softened.

Add the celery and mushrooms and cook for an additional 4–5 minutes, or until all of the vegetables are tender.

Turn off the heat and stir in the egg and grated Parmesan cheese. Season to taste with salt and pepper.

Lay the pastry sheets on a cutting board and, using a ruler and sharp knife, cut each into 9 squares.

Spoon a little of the filling into the center half of the squares and brush the edges of the pastry with butter. Lay another square on top and seal the edges to make a package.

Heat the oil for deep-frying in a heavy-bottom pan to 350°F/180°C, or until a cube of bread browns in 30 seconds. Deep-fry the ravioli, in batches, for 2–3 minutes, or until golden brown. Remove from the oil with a slotted spoon and pat dry on paper towels. Transfer the ravioli to a warmed serving plate and serve at once.

bulgur-filled eggplants

serves 4

1 hour

30 minutes

4 eggplants
salt
generous 1 cup bulgur wheat
1 1/4 cups boiling water
3 tbsp olive oil
2 garlic cloves, crushed
2 tbsp pine nuts
1/2 tsp ground turmeric
1 tsp chili powder

2 celery stalks, chopped
4 scallions, chopped
1 carrot, grated
1 3/4 oz/50 g white mushrooms, chopped
2 tbsp raisins
2 tbsp chopped fresh cilantro

In this recipe, eggplants are filled with a spicy bulgur wheat and vegetable stuffing for a delicious light meal.

Preheat the oven to 350°F/180°C. Using a sharp knife, cut the eggplants in half lengthwise and scoop out the flesh with a teaspoon. Chop the flesh and set aside. Rub the insides of the eggplants with a little salt and let stand for 20 minutes.

Meanwhile, place the bulgur wheat in a large bowl and pour the boiling water over the top. Let stand for 20 minutes, or until all the water has been absorbed.

Heat the oil in a skillet. Add the garlic, pine nuts, turmeric, chili powder, celery, scallions, carrot, mushrooms, and raisins and cook for 2–3 minutes.

Stir in the reserved eggplant flesh and cook for an additional 2–3 minutes. Add the cilantro, mixing well. Remove the skillet from the heat and stir in the bulgur wheat.

Rinse the eggplant shells under cold running water and pat dry with paper towels.

Spoon the bulgur filling into the eggplants and place in a roasting pan. Pour in a little boiling water and cook in the preheated oven for 15–20 minutes. Serve hot.

lentil croquettes

serves 4

10 minutes

55 minutes

2 cups split red lentils, rinsed
1 green bell pepper, finely chopped
1 red onion, finely chopped
2 garlic cloves, crushed
1 tsp garam masala
1/2 tsp chili powder
1 tsp ground cumin
2 tsp lemon juice
2 tbsp chopped unsalted peanuts
2 1/2 cups water

1 egg, beaten
salt and pepper
3 tbsp all-purpose flour, plus extra
   for dusting
1 tsp ground turmeric
1 tsp chili powder
4 tbsp vegetable oil

to serve

salad greens
fresh herbs

These croquettes are ideal served with a crisp salad and a sesame seed paste dip.

cook's tip

Other lentils could be used, but they will require soaking and precooking before use. Split red lentils are used for speed and convenience.

Place the lentils in a large pan with the bell pepper, onion, garlic, garam masala, chili powder, ground cumin, lemon juice, and peanuts.

Add the water and bring to a boil. Lower the heat and let simmer for 30 minutes, or until the liquid has been absorbed, stirring occasionally.

Remove the pan from the heat and let cool slightly. Beat in the egg and season to taste with salt and pepper. Let cool completely.

With floured hands, form the mixture into 8 oblong shapes.

Mix the flour, turmeric, and chili powder together on a small plate. Roll the croquettes in the spiced flour mixture to coat.

Heat the oil in a large skillet and cook the croquettes, in batches, for 10 minutes, turning once, until crisp on both sides. Serve the croquettes with salad greens and fresh herbs.

refried beans
with tortillas

serves 4

15 minutes

15 minutes

beans

2 tbsp olive oil

1 onion, finely chopped

3 garlic cloves, crushed

1 fresh green chile, chopped

14 oz/400 g canned red kidney beans, drained

14 oz/400 g canned pinto beans, drained

2 tbsp chopped fresh cilantro

2/3 cup vegetable stock

8 wheat tortillas

1/4 cup vegetarian Cheddar cheese, grated

salt and pepper

relish

4 scallions, chopped

1 red onion, chopped

1 fresh green chile, chopped

1 tbsp garlic wine vinegar

1 tsp superfine sugar

1 tomato, chopped

Refried beans are a classic Mexican dish and are usually served as an accompaniment. They are, however, delicious when served with warm tortillas and a quick onion relish.

cook's tip

Add a little more liquid to the beans when they are cooking if they start to catch on the bottom of the skillet.

Heat the oil for the beans in a large skillet. Add the onion and sauté for 3–5 minutes. Add the garlic and chile and cook for 1 minute.

Mash the beans with a potato masher and stir into the skillet with the chopped cilantro.

Stir in the stock and cook the beans, stirring constantly, for 5 minutes, or until soft and pulpy.

Place the tortillas on a baking sheet and heat through in a warm oven for 1–2 minutes.

Mix all the relish ingredients together in a serving bowl.

Spoon the beans into a serving dish and top with the cheese. Season well with salt and pepper. Roll the tortillas and serve with the relish and beans.

brown rice, vegetable
& herb gratin

serves 4

15 minutes

1 hour

½ cup brown rice

2 tbsp butter or vegetarian
margarine, plus extra for greasing

1 red onion, chopped

2 garlic cloves, crushed

1 carrot, cut into short thin sticks

1 zucchini, sliced

2¾ oz/75 g baby corn,
halved lengthwise

2 tbsp sunflower seeds

3 tbsp chopped fresh mixed herbs

scant 1 cup grated mozzarella cheese

salt and pepper

2 tbsp fresh whole-wheat bread
crumbs

*This is a really filling dish
and does not require
an accompaniment. It is very
versatile, and could be made with
a wide selection of vegetables.*

cook's tip

*Use an alternative rice, such as
basmati, and flavor the dish with
curry spices, if you prefer.*

Preheat the oven to 350°F/180°C. Cook the rice in a large pan of boiling salted water for 20 minutes. Drain well.

Lightly grease a 3½-cup ovenproof dish.

Heat the butter in a skillet. Add the onion and cook, stirring constantly, for 2 minutes, or until softened.

Add the garlic, carrot, zucchini, and baby corn and cook for an additional 5 minutes, stirring.

Mix the rice with the sunflower seeds and mixed herbs in a bowl and stir into the skillet.

Stir in half of the grated mozzarella cheese and season to taste with salt and pepper.

Spoon the mixture into the greased dish and top with the bread crumbs and remaining cheese. Cook in the preheated oven for 25–30 minutes, or until the cheese starts to turn golden. Serve.

green lentil &
mixed vegetable pan-fry

serves 4

30 minutes

45 minutes

1³⁄₈ cups green lentils

4 tbsp butter or vegetarian margarine

2 garlic cloves, crushed

2 tbsp olive oil

1 tbsp cider vinegar

1 red onion, cut into 8 pieces

1³⁄₄ oz/50 g baby corn, halved lengthwise

1 yellow bell pepper, seeded and cut into strips

1 red bell pepper, seeded and cut into strips

1³⁄₄ oz/50 g green beans, halved

½ cup vegetable stock

2 tbsp honey

salt and pepper

The green lentils used in this recipe require soaking, but are worth it for the flavor. If time is short, use split dried field peas, which do not require soaking.

variation

This pan-fry is very versatile—you can use a mixture of your favorite vegetables, if you prefer. Try zucchini, carrots, or snow peas.

Soak the lentils in a large pan of cold water for 25 minutes. Bring to a boil, lower the heat, and let simmer for 20 minutes. Drain thoroughly.

Add 1 tablespoon of the butter, 1 garlic clove, 1 tablespoon of oil, and the vinegar to the lentils and mix well.

Melt the remaining butter, garlic, and oil in a skillet. Add the onion, baby corn, bell peppers, and beans and stir-fry for 3–4 minutes.

Add the stock and bring to a boil for 10 minutes, or until all the liquid has evaporated.

Add the honey and season to taste with salt and pepper. Stir in the lentil mixture and cook for 1 minute to heat through. Spoon onto warmed serving plates and serve.

falafel

serves 4

25 minutes

10–15 minutes

1 lb 7 oz/650 g canned chickpeas, drained

1 red onion, chopped

3 garlic cloves, crushed

3½ oz/100 g whole-wheat bread

2 small fresh red chiles

1 tsp ground cumin

1 tsp ground coriander

½ tsp ground turmeric

1 tbsp chopped fresh cilantro, plus extra to garnish

salt and pepper

1 egg, beaten

1¾ cups fresh whole-wheat bread crumbs

vegetable oil, for deep-frying

lemon wedges, to garnish

tomato and cucumber salad, to serve

These are a very tasty, well-known Middle Eastern dish of small chickpea-based balls, spiced and deep-fried. They are delicious hot with a crisp tomato salad.

cook's tip

Serve the falafel with a cilantro and yogurt sauce. Mix ⅓ cup plain yogurt with 2 tablespoons chopped fresh cilantro and 1 crushed garlic clove.

Place the chickpeas, onion, garlic, bread, chiles, spices, and fresh cilantro in a food processor and process for 30 seconds. Stir and season well with salt and pepper. Remove the mixture from the food processor and shape into walnut-size balls.

Place the beaten egg in a shallow bowl and place the whole-wheat bread crumbs on a plate. Dip the balls into the egg to coat, then roll them in the bread crumbs, shaking off any excess.

Heat the oil for deep-frying in a large, heavy-bottom pan to 350°F/180°C, or until a cube of bread browns in 30 seconds. Deep-fry the falafel, in batches, for 2–3 minutes, or until crisp and browned.

Remove the falafels from the oil with a slotted spoon and dry on paper towels. Garnish with chopped cilantro and lemon wedges and serve with a cucumber and tomato salad.

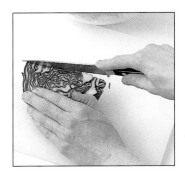

cabbage & walnut stir-fry

serves 4

10 minutes

10 minutes

12 oz/350 g white cabbage
12 oz/350 g red cabbage
4 tbsp peanut oil
1 tbsp walnut oil
2 garlic cloves, crushed
8 scallions, trimmed

8 oz/225 g firm tofu, cubed
  (drained weight)
2 tbsp lemon juice
scant 1 cup walnut halves
2 tsp Dijon mustard
salt and pepper
2 tsp poppy seeds

This is a really quick, one-pan dish using white and red cabbage for color and flavor.

cook's tip

As well as adding protein, vitamins, and useful fats to the diet, nuts and seeds add flavor and texture to vegetarian meals. Keep a good supply of them in your pantry because they can be used in a variety of dishes—salads, bakes, stir-fries to name but a few.

Using a sharp knife, shred the white and red cabbages thinly and set aside until required.

Heat the peanut and walnut oils in a preheated wok. Add the garlic, cabbage, scallions, and tofu and cook for 5 minutes, stirring.

Add the lemon juice, walnuts, and mustard, then season to taste with salt and pepper and cook for an additional 5 minutes, or until the cabbage is tender.

Transfer the stir-fry to a warmed serving bowl, sprinkle with poppy seeds, and serve.

spinach frittata

serves 4

20 minutes

20 minutes

1 lb/450 g fresh spinach leaves
2 tsp water
4 eggs, beaten
2 tbsp light cream
2 garlic cloves, crushed
1¾ oz/50 g canned corn, drained
1 celery stalk, chopped
1 fresh red chile, chopped
2 tomatoes, seeded and diced

2 tbsp olive oil
2 tbsp butter
¼ cup pecan halves
2 tbsp grated romano cheese
1 oz/25 g fontina cheese, cubed
pinch of paprika

A frittata is another word for a large, thick omelet. This is an Italian dish, which may be made with many flavorings. Spinach is used as the main ingredient in this recipe for color and flavor.

Cook the spinach in the water in a covered pan for 5 minutes. Drain thoroughly and pat dry on paper towels.

Beat the eggs in a bowl and stir in the spinach, cream, garlic, corn, celery, chile, and tomatoes. Mix well.

Heat the oil and butter in an 8-inch/20-cm heavy-bottom skillet.

Spoon the egg mixture into the skillet and sprinkle with the pecan halves, romano and fontina cheeses, and paprika. Cook, without stirring, over medium heat for 5–7 minutes, or until the underside is brown.

Place a large plate over the skillet and invert to turn out the frittata. Slide it back into the skillet and cook the other side for an additional 2–3 minutes. Serve the frittata straight from the skillet. Alternatively, transfer to a serving plate.

  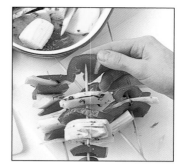

marinated broiled
fennel

 serves 4

 1 hour 15 minutes

 10 minutes

2 fennel bulbs
1 red bell pepper, seeded and cut
  into large pieces
1 lime, cut into 8 wedges
fennel fronds, to garnish
crisp salad, to serve (optional)

marinade

2 tbsp lime juice
4 tbsp olive oil
2 garlic cloves, crushed
1 tsp whole-grain mustard
1 tbsp chopped fresh thyme

Fennel has a wonderful anise flavor, which is ideal for broiling or barbecuing. Marinated in lime, garlic, oil, and mustard, this recipe is really delicious.

cook's tip

Soak the wooden skewers in water for 20 minutes before using to prevent them burning during cooking.

Using a sharp knife, cut each of the fennel bulbs into 8 pieces and place in a shallow dish. Mix in the bell pepper.

To make the marinade, mix the lime juice, oil, garlic, mustard, and thyme together in a measuring cup or pitcher. Pour the marinade over the fennel and bell pepper, then cover and let marinate for 1 hour.

Preheat the broiler to medium. Thread the fennel and bell pepper onto presoaked wooden skewers with the lime wedges and cook the kabobs under the hot broiler for 10 minutes, turning and basting frequently with the marinade.

Transfer to serving plates, garnish with fennel fronds, and serve with a crisp salad, if you like.

ciabatta rolls

serves 4

20 minutes

10 minutes

4 ciabatta rolls
2 tbsp olive oil
1 garlic clove crushed
filling
1 red bell pepper

1 green bell pepper
1 yellow bell pepper
4 radishes, sliced
1 bunch of watercress
generous $3/8$ cup cream cheese

Sandwiches are always a welcome snack, but can be quite mundane. These crisp ciabatta rolls filled with roast bell peppers and cheese are irresistible and will always be a popular light meal.

cook's tip

To peel bell peppers, place them in a plastic bag after broiling. This traps the steam, loosening the skins, and making them easier to peel.

Preheat the broiler to medium. Slice the ciabatta rolls in half. Heat the oil and crushed garlic in a pan. Pour the garlic and oil mixture over the cut surfaces of the rolls and let stand until required.

To make the filling, halve the bell peppers and place, skin-side uppermost, on a broiler rack. Cook under the hot broiler for 8–10 minutes, or until just starting to char. Remove the bell peppers from the broiler and let stand until cool enough to handle. Peel and slice thinly.

Arrange the radish slices on one half of each roll with a few watercress leaves. Spoon the cream cheese on top. Pile the bell peppers on top of the cream cheese and top with the other half of the roll. Serve.

main meals

This is the most comprehensive chapter in the book, being perhaps the most important. In a vegetarian diet it is essential to eat a good balance of foods and the following recipes make use of beans, grains, tofu, and vegetables to aid in this quest. The recipes in this chapter will enable you to build a balanced, nutritious, and flavorful menu, which will meet all of your needs.

Anyone who ever thought that vegetarian meals were dull will be proved wrong by the rich variety of dishes in this chapter. You'll recognize influences from Indian, Mexican, and Chinese cooking, but there are also traditional stews and casseroles as well as hearty bakes and roasts. They all make exciting eating at any time of year, at virtually any occasion. There are ideas for midweek meals or for entertaining, some traditional and some more unusual. There is no reason why you cannot enjoy experimenting and adding your own touch to these imaginative ideas.

mushroom & spinach puff pastry

 serves 4

 20 minutes

 30 minutes

2 tbsp butter
1 red onion, halved and sliced
2 garlic cloves, crushed
8 oz/225 g open-cap mushrooms, sliced
3¾ cups fresh baby spinach leaves

pinch of nutmeg
4 tbsp heavy cream
salt and pepper
8 oz/225 g ready-made puff pastry
all-purpose flour, for dusting
1 egg, beaten
2 tsp poppy seeds

These puff packages are easy to make and delicious to eat. Filled with garlic, mushrooms, and spinach they are ideal with a fresh tomato or cheese sauce.

Preheat the oven to 400°F/200°C. Melt the butter in a large skillet. Add the onion and garlic and sauté for 3–4 minutes, stirring well, until the onion has softened.

Add the mushrooms, spinach, and nutmeg and cook for an additional 2–3 minutes.

Stir in the heavy cream, mixing well. Season to taste with salt and pepper and remove the skillet from the heat.

Roll the puff pastry out on a lightly floured counter and cut into 4 × 6-inch/15-cm circles.

Spoon one-quarter of the filling onto one half of each circle and fold the pastry over to encase the filling. Press down to seal the edges of the pastry and brush with the beaten egg. Sprinkle with the poppy seeds.

Place the packages onto a dampened baking sheet and cook in the preheated oven for 20 minutes, or until risen and golden brown.

Transfer the mushroom and spinach puff pastry packages to serving plates and serve at once.

cook's tip

The baking sheet is dampened so that steam forms with the heat of the oven and helps the pastry to rise and set.

chickpea roast
with sherry sauce

 serves 4

 20 minutes

45 minutes

1 lb/450 g canned chickpeas, drained
1 tsp yeast extract
generous 1 cup chopped walnuts
2¾ cups fresh white bread crumbs
1 onion, finely chopped
3½ oz/100 g mushrooms, sliced
1¾ oz/50 g canned corn, drained
2 garlic cloves, crushed
2 tbsp dry sherry
2 tbsp vegetable stock
1 tbsp chopped fresh cilantro
salt and pepper

8 oz/225 g ready-made puff pastry
all-purpose flour, for dusting
1 egg, beaten
2 tbsp milk

sauce
1 tbsp vegetable oil
1 leek, thinly sliced
4 tbsp dry sherry
⅔ cup vegetable stock

This is a vegetarian version of the classic "Beef Wellington," and just as delicious. Served with a sherry sauce and roast vegetables it makes a tasty and impressive main dish.

Preheat the oven to 400°F/200°C. Place the chickpeas, yeast extract, nuts, and bread crumbs in a food processor and process for 30 seconds. Sauté the onion and mushrooms in their own juices in a large skillet for 3–4 minutes. Stir in the chickpea mixture, corn, and garlic. Add the sherry, stock, cilantro, and season to taste with salt and pepper. Bind the mixture together, then remove the skillet from the heat and let cool.

Roll the pastry out on a floured counter to form a 14-inch/35-cm x 12-inch/30-cm rectangle. Form the chickpea mixture into a loaf shape and wrap the pastry round it, sealing the edges. Place seam-side down on a dampened baking sheet and score the top in a criss-cross pattern. Mix the egg and milk together and brush over the pastry. Cook in the preheated oven for 25–30 minutes.

Heat the oil for the sauce in a small pan. Add the leek and sauté for 5 minutes. Add the sherry and stock, bring to a boil, then let simmer for 5 minutes. Serve with the roast.

kidney bean kiev

serves 4

25 minutes

20 minutes

garlic butter
3 ½ oz/100 g butter
3 garlic cloves, crushed
1 tbsp chopped fresh parsley

bean patties
1 lb 7 oz/650 g canned red kidney
  beans, drained and rinsed
2 ¾ cups fresh white bread crumbs

2 tbsp butter
1 leek, chopped
1 celery stalk, chopped
1 tbsp chopped fresh parsley
salt and pepper
1 egg, beaten
vegetable oil, for pan-frying

This is a vegetarian version of chicken kiev, the bean patties taking the place of the chicken. Topped with garlic and herb butter and coated in bread crumbs, this version is just as delicious.

To make the garlic butter, place the butter, garlic, and parsley in a bowl and blend together with a wooden spoon. Place the garlic butter mixture on a sheet of parchment paper and roll into a cigar shape, then wrap in the parchment paper. Let chill in the refrigerator until required.

Using a potato masher, mash the red kidney beans in a large bowl and stir in 1⅜ cups of the bread crumbs until thoroughly blended.

Melt the butter in a large skillet. Add the leek and celery and sauté for 3–4 minutes, stirring.

Add the bean mixture to the skillet together with the parsley. Season to taste with salt and pepper and mix well. Remove the skillet from the heat and let cool slightly.

Form the bean mixture into 4 equal-size ovals.

Slice the chilled garlic butter into 4 portions and place a slice in the center of each bean patty. Mold the bean mixture round the garlic butter to encase it completely.

Dip each bean patty into the beaten egg to coat and then roll in the remaining bread crumbs.

Heat a little oil in a skillet and pan-fry the bean patties, turning once, for 7–10 minutes, or until golden. Serve.

cashew paella

serves 4

15 minutes

35 minutes

2 tbsp olive oil
1 tbsp butter
1 red onion, chopped
scant ¾ cup Arborio rice
1 tsp ground turmeric
1 tsp ground cumin
½ tsp chili powder
3 garlic cloves, crushed
1 fresh green chile, sliced
1 green bell pepper, diced
1 red bell pepper, diced
2¾ oz/75 g baby corn,
    halved lengthwise

2 tbsp pitted black olives
1 large tomato, seeded and diced
2 cups vegetable stock
½ cup unsalted cashews
¼ cup frozen peas
salt and pepper
2 tbsp chopped fresh parsley
pinch of cayenne pepper
fresh herbs, to garnish

Paella traditionally contains chicken and fish, but this recipe is packed with vegetables and nuts for a truly delicious and simple vegetarian dish.

cook's tip

For authenticity and flavor, use a few saffron threads soaked in a little boiling water instead of the ground turmeric. Saffron has a lovely, nutty flavor.

Heat the oil and butter in a large skillet or paella pan until the butter has melted.

Add the chopped onion to the skillet and sauté for 2–3 minutes, stirring constantly, until the onion has softened.

Stir in the rice, turmeric, cumin, chili powder, garlic, chile, bell peppers, baby corn, olives, and tomato and cook over medium heat for 1–2 minutes, stirring occasionally.

Pour in the stock and bring the mixture to a boil. Lower the heat and cook for 20 minutes, stirring.

Add the cashews and peas to the mixture in the skillet and cook for an additional 5 minutes, stirring occasionally. Season to taste with salt and pepper and sprinkle with parsley and cayenne pepper. Transfer to warmed serving plates, garnish with fresh herbs, and serve at once.

vegetable & tofu strudels

serves 4

25 minutes

30 minutes

12 sheets phyllo pastry

2 tbsp butter or vegetarian margarine, melted, plus extra for greasing

crisp salad, to serve

filling

2 tbsp vegetable oil

2 tbsp butter or vegetarian margarine

5½ oz/150 g potatoes finely diced

1 leek, shredded

2 garlic cloves, crushed

1 tsp garam masala

½ tsp chili powder

½ tsp ground turmeric

1¾ oz/50 g okra, sliced

3½ oz/100 g white mushrooms, sliced

2 tomatoes, diced

8 oz/225 g firm tofu, diced (drained weight)

salt and pepper

These strudels look really impressive and are perfect if friends are coming round or served as part of a formal dinner party dish.

cook's tip

Decorate the outside of the strudels with crumpled pastry trimmings before cooking for an impressive effect.

Preheat the oven to 375°F/190°C. To make the filling, heat the oil and butter in a skillet. Add the potatoes and leek and cook for 2–3 minutes, stirring constantly.

Add the garlic and spices, okra, mushrooms, tomatoes, tofu, and season to taste with salt and pepper. Cook, stirring, for 5–7 minutes, or until tender.

Lay the pastry out on a cutting board and brush each individual sheet with melted butter. Place 3 sheets on top of one another and repeat to make 4 stacks.

Spoon one-quarter of the filling along the center of each stack and brush the edges with a little melted butter. Fold the short edges in and roll up lengthwise to form a cigar shape. Brush the outside with melted butter. Place the strudels on a greased baking sheet.

Cook the strudels in the preheated oven for 20 minutes, or until golden brown. Serve at once with a crisp salad.

vegetable lasagna

serves 4

35 minutes

55 minutes

1 eggplant, sliced
salt and pepper
3 tbsp olive oil
2 garlic cloves, crushed
1 red onion, halved and sliced
1 green bell pepper, diced
1 red bell pepper, diced
1 yellow bell pepper, diced
8 oz/225 g mixed mushrooms, sliced
2 celery stalks, sliced
1 zucchini, diced
1/2 tsp chili powder
1/2 tsp ground cumin
2 tomatoes, chopped

1 1/4 cups strained tomatoes
2 tbsp chopped fresh basil
8 no precook lasagna verdi sheets

cheese sauce

2 tbsp butter or vegetarian
  margarine
1 tbsp flour
2/3 cup vegetable stock
1 1/4 cups milk
scant 3/4 cup vegetarian Cheddar
  cheese, grated
1 tsp Dijon mustard
1 tbsp chopped fresh basil
1 egg, beaten

This colorful and tasty lasagna, with layers of vegetables in tomato sauce and eggplant, all topped with a rich cheese sauce is just simply delicious.

Preheat the oven to 350°F/180°C. Place the eggplant slices in a strainer, sprinkle with salt, and let stand for 20 minutes. Rinse under cold running water, drain, and set aside.

Heat the oil in a large skillet. Add the garlic and onion and sauté for 1–2 minutes. Add the bell peppers, mushrooms, celery, and zucchini and cook for 3–4 minutes, stirring. Stir in the spices and cook for 1 minute.

Mix the chopped tomatoes, strained tomatoes, and basil together, then season well with salt and pepper.

To make the sauce, melt the butter in a pan. Add the flour and cook for 1 minute. Remove the pan from the heat and stir in the stock and milk. Return to the heat and add half the cheese and mustard. Boil, stirring, until thickened. Stir in the basil and season to taste with salt and pepper. Remove the pan from the heat and stir in the egg. Place half of the lasagna sheets in an ovenproof dish. Top with half of the vegetables, then half of the tomato sauce. Cover with half the eggplant. Repeat and spoon the cheese sauce on top. Sprinkle with cheese and cook in the preheated oven for 40 minutes. Serve.

lentil & rice

casserole

serves 4

15 minutes

40 minutes

2 cups split red lentils, rinsed
1/4 cup long-grain white rice
4 cups vegetable stock
2/3 cup dry white wine
1 leek, cut into chunks
3 garlic cloves, crushed
14 oz/400 g canned chopped
  tomatoes
1 tsp ground cumin

1 tsp chili powder
1 tsp garam masala
1 red bell pepper, sliced
3 1/2 oz/100 g small broccoli florets
8 baby corn, halved lengthwise
1 3/4 oz/50 g green beans, halved
1 tbsp fresh basil, shredded
salt and pepper
fresh basil sprigs, to garnish

*This is a hearty dish,
perfect for cold days when a filling
hot dish is just what you need.*

variation

*You can vary the rice in this
recipe—use brown or wild
rice, if you prefer.*

Place the lentils, rice, stock, and white wine in an ovenproof casserole and
cook over low heat for 20 minutes, stirring occasionally.

Add the leek, garlic, tomatoes, cumin, chili powder, garam masala, bell
pepper, broccoli, baby corn, and green beans.

Bring the mixture to a boil, lower the heat, cover, and let simmer for an
additional 10–15 minutes, or until the vegetables are tender.

Add the shredded basil and season to taste with salt and pepper.

Garnish with fresh basil sprigs and serve at once.

vegetable hotchpotch

serves 4

25 minutes

1 hour

2 large potatoes, thinly sliced
2 tbsp vegetable oil
1 red onion, halved and sliced
1 leek, sliced
2 garlic cloves, crushed
1 carrot, cut into chunks
3 1/2 oz/100 g broccoli florets
3 1/2 oz/100 g cauliflower florets
2 small turnips, quartered
1 tbsp all-purpose flour

3 cups vegetable stock
2/3 cup dry cider
1 eating apple, sliced
2 tbsp chopped fresh sage
pinch of cayenne pepper
salt and pepper
scant 1/2 cup vegetarian Cheddar
cheese, grated

In this recipe, a variety of vegetables are cooked under a layer of potatoes, topped with cheese, and cooked until golden brown for a filling and tasty meal.

cook's tip

If the potato starts to brown too quickly, cover with foil for the last 10 minutes of the cooking time to prevent the top burning.

Preheat the oven to 375°F/190°C. Cook the potato slices in a pan of boiling water for 10 minutes. Drain thoroughly and set aside until required.

Heat the oil in an ovenproof casserole. Add the onion, leek, and garlic and sauté for 2–3 minutes. Add the remaining vegetables and cook for an additional 3–4 minutes, stirring.

Stir in the flour and cook for 1 minute. Gradually add the stock and cider and bring the mixture to a boil. Add the apple, sage, and cayenne and season well with salt and pepper. Remove the casserole from the heat. Transfer the vegetables to an ovenproof dish.

Arrange the potato slices on top of the vegetable mixture to cover.

Sprinkle the cheese on top of the potato slices and cook in the preheated oven for 30–35 minutes, or until the potato is golden brown and starting to crisp slightly round the edges. Serve at once.

vegetable chop suey

serves 4

10 minutes

6 minutes

2 tbsp peanut oil
1 onion, chopped
3 garlic cloves, chopped
1 green bell pepper, diced
1 red bell pepper, diced
2¾ oz/75 g broccoli florets
1 zucchini, sliced
1 oz/25 g green beans

1 carrot, cut into short thin sticks
²/3 cup bean sprouts
2 tsp light brown sugar
2 tbsp light soy sauce
½ cup vegetable stock
salt and pepper
freshly cooked noodles, to serve

A classic Chinese dish found on all takeout menus, this recipe is quick to prepare and makes a tasty meal.

Heat the oil in a preheated wok until almost smoking. Add the onion and garlic and stir-fry for 30 seconds.

Stir in the bell peppers, broccoli, zucchini, beans, and carrot and stir-fry for an additional 2–3 minutes.

Add the bean sprouts, sugar, soy sauce, and stock. Season to taste with salt and pepper and cook for 2 minutes.

Transfer the vegetables to individual serving plates and serve at once with freshly cooked noodles.

cook's tip

The clever design of a wok, with its spherical bottom and high sloping sides, enables the food to be tossed so that it is cooked quickly and evenly. It is essential to heat the wok sufficiently before you add the ingredients to ensure quick and even cooking.

Ensure that the vegetable pieces are the same size to make sure that they all cook in the time.

variation

Add 1 tablespoon chili oil for a hotter flavor and add cashews for extra crunch.

vegetable
toad-in-the-hole

serves 4

15 minutes

55 minutes

batter
2/3 cup all-purpose flour
pinch of salt
2 eggs, beaten
scant 1 cup milk
2 tbsp whole-grain mustard
2 tbsp vegetable oil

filling
2 tbsp butter
2 garlic cloves, crushed

1 onion, cut into 8 wedges
2¾ oz/75 g baby carrots, halved
  lengthwise
1¾ oz/50 g green beans
1¾ oz/50 g canned corn, drained
2 tomatoes, seeded and cut
  into chunks
1 tsp whole-grain mustard
1 tbsp chopped fresh mixed herbs
salt and pepper

*This dish can be made in
one large dish or in individual
Yorkshire pudding pans or
muffin pans.*

cook's tip

*It is important that the oil
is hot before adding the batter
so that the batter starts to cook
and rise immediately.*

Preheat the oven to 400°F/200°C. To make the batter, sift the flour and the salt into a large bowl. Make a well in the center and beat in the eggs and milk to form a batter. Stir in the mustard and let stand until required.

Pour the oil into a shallow ovenproof dish and heat in the preheated oven for 10 minutes.

To make the filling, cook the carrots and beans in a pan of boiling water for 7 minutes, or until tender. Drain well. Melt the butter in a skillet. Add the garlic and onion and sauté for 2 minutes, stirring.

Add the corn and tomatoes to the skillet with the mustard and herbs. Season well with salt and pepper and add the carrots and beans.

Remove the dish from the oven and pour in the batter. Spoon the vegetables into the center, return to the oven, and cook for 30–35 minutes, or until the batter has risen and set. Serve at once.

vegetable jalousie

serves 4

25 minutes

45 minutes

1 lb/450 g ready-made puff pastry
all-purpose flour, for dusting
1 egg, beaten

filling

2 tbsp butter or vegetarian
    margarine
1 leek, shredded
2 garlic cloves, crushed
1 red bell pepper, sliced

1 yellow bell pepper, sliced
1¾ oz/50 g mushrooms, sliced
2¾ oz/75 g small asparagus spears
2 tbsp all-purpose flour
⅓ cup vegetable stock
⅓ cup milk
4 tbsp dry white wine
1 tbsp chopped fresh oregano
salt and pepper

This is a very easy dish to make, but looks impressive. The mixture of vegetables gives the dish a wonderful color and flavor.

Preheat the oven to 400°F/200°C. To make the filling, melt the butter in a pan. Add the leek and garlic and sauté for 2 minutes, stirring. Add the remaining vegetables and cook, stirring, for 3–4 minutes.

Add the flour and cook for 1 minute, then remove the pan from the heat and stir in the stock, milk, and white wine. Return the pan to the heat and bring to a boil, stirring, until thickened. Stir in the chopped oregano and season to taste with salt and pepper.

Roll half of the puff pastry out on a lightly floured counter to form a rectangle 16½ inches x 6 inches/42 cm x 15 cm.

Roll out the other half of the puff pastry to the same shape, but a little larger. Place the smaller rectangle on a baking sheet lined with dampened parchment paper.

Spoon the filling on top of the smaller rectangle, leaving a ½-inch/1-cm clean edge. Cut parallel slits across the larger rectangle to within 1 inch/ 2.5 cm of each edge.

Brush the edge of the smaller rectangle with egg and, using a rolling pin, place the larger rectangle on top, sealing the edges well.

Brush the whole jalousie with egg and cook in the preheated oven for 30–35 minutes, or until risen and golden brown. Serve at once.

cauliflower, broccoli
& cheese tart

serves 8

15 minutes

50 minutes

pie dough

1 1/8 cups all-purpose flour, plus extra
    for dusting
pinch of salt
1/2 tsp paprika
1 tsp dried thyme
2 3/4 oz/75 g vegetarian margarine
3 tbsp water

filling

3 1/2 oz/100 g cauliflower florets
3 1/2 oz/100 g broccoli florets
1 onion, cut into 8 wedges

2 tbsp butter or vegetarian
    margarine
1 tbsp all-purpose flour
1/3 cup vegetable stock
1/2 cup milk
scant 3/4 cup vegetarian Cheddar
    cheese, grated
salt and pepper
paprika, for dusting

*This really is a tasty tart, the pastry
shell may be made in advance and
frozen until required.*

Preheat the oven to 375°F/190°C. To make the pie dough, sift the flour
and salt into a large bowl. Add the paprika and thyme and rub in the
margarine. Stir in the water and bind to form a dough.

Roll the dough out on a floured counter and use to line a 7-inch/18-cm
loose-bottom tart pan. Prick the base with a fork and line with parchment
paper. Fill with ceramic baking beans or pie weights and bake in the
preheated oven for 15 minutes. Remove the parchment paper and beans
and return the pastry shell to the oven for 5 minutes.

To make the filling, cook the vegetables in a pan of boiling water for
10–12 minutes, until tender. Drain and set aside.

Melt the butter in a small pan. Add the flour and cook, stirring
constantly, for 1 minute. Remove the pan from the heat, stir in the stock
and milk, and return to the heat. Bring to a boil, stirring, then add scant
1/2 cup of the cheese. Season to taste with salt and pepper.

Spoon the cauliflower, broccoli, and onion into the pastry shell. Pour over
the sauce and sprinkle with the remaining cheese. Return to the oven for
10 minutes, or until the cheese is bubbling. Dust with paprika and serve.

roast bell pepper tart

 serves 8

 25 minutes

40 minutes

pie dough

1 ⅛ cups all-purpose flour, plus extra for dusting

pinch of salt

2¾ oz/75 g butter or vegetarian margarine

2 tbsp green pitted olives, finely chopped

3 tbsp cold water

filling

1 red bell pepper

1 green bell pepper

1 yellow bell pepper

2 garlic cloves, crushed

2 tbsp olive oil

⅞ cup mozzarella cheese, grated

2 eggs

⅔ cup milk

1 tbsp chopped fresh basil

salt and pepper

This tastes truly delicious, because the flavor of roasted vegetables is completely different from that of boiled or cooked.

cook's tip

Make sure that the olives are very finely chopped, otherwise they will make holes in the pie dough.

Preheat the oven to 400°F/200°C. To make the pie dough, sift the flour and salt into a large bowl. Add the butter and rub it in until the mixture resembles bread crumbs. Add the olives and cold water and bring the mixture together to form a dough.

Roll the dough out on to a floured counter and use to line an 8-inch/20-cm loose-bottom tart pan. Prick the base with a fork and let chill until required.

Using a sharp knife, cut the bell peppers in half lengthwise and lay skin-side uppermost on a baking sheet. Mix the garlic and oil together and brush over the bell peppers. Cook in the preheated oven for 20 minutes, or until starting to char slightly. Remove the bell peppers from the oven and let cool slightly, then thinly slice. Arrange in the base of the pastry shell, layering with the mozzarella cheese.

Beat the egg and milk together in a measuring cup or pitcher and add the basil. Season to taste with salt and pepper and pour over the bell peppers. Place the tart on a baking sheet and return to the oven for 20 minutes, or until set. Serve either hot or cold.

vegetable biryani

serves 4

2 hours 15 minutes

1 hour 5 minutes

1 large potato, cubed
3½ oz/100 g baby carrots
1¾ oz/50 g okra, thickly sliced
2 celery stalks, sliced
2¾ oz/75 g baby white mushrooms, halved
1 eggplant, halved and sliced
1¼ cups plain yogurt
1 tbsp grated fresh gingerroot

2 large onions, grated
4 garlic cloves, crushed
1 tsp ground turmeric
1 tbsp curry powder
2 tbsp butter
2 onions, sliced
generous 1 cup basmati rice
fresh cilantro leaves, to garnish

The biryani originated in the North of India, and was a dish reserved for festivals. The vegetables are marinated in a yogurt-based marinade and cooked in a casserole with the rice and onions.

Cook the potato cubes, carrots, and okra in a pan of boiling salted water for 7–8 minutes. Drain well and place in a large bowl. Mix with the celery, mushrooms, and eggplant.

Mix the yogurt, ginger, grated onions, garlic, turmeric, and curry powder together in a separate bowl and spoon over the vegetables. Cover and let marinate in the refrigerator for at least 2 hours.

Preheat the oven to 375°F/190°C. Heat the butter in a skillet. Add the sliced onions and cook for 5–6 minutes, or until golden. Remove a few onions from the skillet and set aside for the garnish.

Cook the rice in a pan of boiling water for 7 minutes. Drain well.

Add the marinated vegetables to the onions and cook for 10 minutes.

Place half of the rice in an 8-cup ovenproof casserole. Spoon the vegetables on top and cover with the remaining rice. Cover and cook in the preheated oven for 20–25 minutes, or until the rice is tender.

Spoon the biryani onto a serving plate, garnish with the reserved onions and cilantro leaves, and serve at once.

baked **cheese** & tomato macaroni

serves 4

15 minutes

35–40 minutes

8 oz/225 g dried elbow macaroni

1 ½ cups grated vegetarian Cheddar cheese

scant 1 cup freshly grated Parmesan cheese

1 tbsp butter or vegetarian margarine, plus extra for greasing

4 tbsp fresh white bread crumbs

1 tbsp chopped fresh basil

tomato sauce

1 tbsp olive oil

1 shallot, finely chopped

2 garlic cloves, crushed

1 lb/450 g canned chopped tomatoes

1 tbsp chopped fresh basil

salt and pepper

This is a simple, family dish which is easy to prepare and cook. Serve with a salad, if you like.

Preheat the oven to 375°F/190°C. To make the tomato sauce, heat the oil in a pan. Add the chopped shallot and garlic and sauté for 1 minute. Add the tomatoes, basil, salt, and pepper to taste and cook over medium heat, stirring, for 10 minutes.

Meanwhile, cook the macaroni in a large pan of boiling salted water for 8 minutes, or until just undercooked. Drain.

Mix both of the cheeses together in a bowl.

Grease a deep, ovenproof dish. Spoon a third of the tomato sauce into the base of the dish, top with a third of the macaroni and then a third of the cheeses. Season to taste with salt and pepper. Repeat the layers twice.

Mix the bread crumbs and basil together and sprinkle over the top. Dot with the butter and cook in the preheated oven for 25 minutes, or until golden brown and bubbling. Serve.

cook's tip

Use other dried pasta shapes, such as penne, if you have them to hand, instead of the macaroni.

chickpea
& vegetable casserole

serves 4

15 minutes

40 minutes

1 tbsp olive oil
1 red onion, halved and sliced
3 garlic cloves, crushed
5 cups fresh spinach leaves
1 fennel bulb, cut into 8 pieces
1 red bell pepper, cubed
1 tbsp all-purpose flour
2 cups vegetable stock
1/3 cup dry white wine

14 oz/400 g canned chickpeas, drained
1 bay leaf
1 tsp ground coriander
1/2 tsp paprika
salt and pepper
fennel fronds, to garnish

This hearty dish is best served with warm crusty bread to mop up the delicious juices.

Heat the oil in a large ovenproof casserole. Add the onion and garlic and sauté for 1 minute, stirring. Add the spinach and cook for 4 minutes, or until wilted.

Add the fennel and bell pepper and cook for 2 minutes, stirring.

Stir in the flour and cook for 1 minute.

Add the stock, wine, chickpeas, bay leaf, coriander, and paprika, cover, and cook for 30 minutes. Season to taste with salt and pepper, garnish with fennel fronds, and serve at once.

cook's tip

Use other canned beans instead of the chickpeas, if you prefer.

variation

Replace the coriander with nutmeg, if you prefer, as it works particularly well with spinach.

sweet & sour
vegetables & tofu

serves 4

10 minutes

15 minutes

1 tbsp peanut oil	1¾ oz/50 g canned bamboo shoots
2 garlic cloves, crushed	8 oz/225 g marinated firm tofu, cubed
1 tsp grated fresh gingerroot	2 tbsp dry sherry
1¾ oz/50 g baby corn	2 tbsp rice vinegar
1¾ oz/50 g snow peas	2 tbsp honey
1 carrot, cut into short thin sticks	1 tbsp light soy sauce
1 green bell pepper, cut into short thin sticks	⅔ cup vegetable stock
8 scallions, trimmed	1 tbsp cornstarch

Serve this dish with plain noodles or fluffy white rice for a filling Asian meal.

variation

You can replace any of the vegetables in this dish with others of your choice. For a colorful, attractive stir-fry, select vegetables with bright, contrasting colors.

Heat the oil in a preheated wok until almost smoking.

Add the garlic and ginger and cook for 30 seconds, stirring frequently.

Add the baby corn, snow peas, carrot, and bell pepper and stir-fry for 5 minutes, or until the vegetables are tender.

Add the scallions, bamboo shoots, and tofu and stir-fry for an additional 2 minutes.

Stir in the sherry, rice vinegar, honey, soy sauce, stock, and cornstarch and bring to a boil. Lower the heat and let simmer for 2 minutes. Transfer to serving dishes and serve at once.

spicy potato & lemon casserole

serves 4

15 minutes

35 minutes

generous ⅓ cup olive oil
2 red onions, cut into 8 wedges
3 garlic cloves, crushed
2 tsp ground cumin
2 tsp ground coriander
pinch of cayenne pepper
1 carrot, thickly sliced
2 small turnips, quartered

1 zucchini, sliced
1 lb/450 g potatoes, thickly sliced
juice and zest of 2 large lemons
1¼ cups vegetable stock
salt and pepper
2 tbsp chopped fresh cilantro

This is based on a Moroccan dish in which potatoes are spiced with coriander and cumin and cooked in a lemon sauce.

cook's tip

A selection of spices and herbs is important for adding variety to your cooking—add to your range each time you try a new recipe.

Check the vegetables while cooking, because they may start to stick to the casserole. Add a little more boiling water or stock if necessary.

Heat the oil in an ovenproof casserole.

Add the onion wedges and sauté for 3 minutes, stirring.

Add the garlic and cook for 30 seconds. Mix in the spices and cook for 1 minute, stirring constantly.

Add the carrot, turnips, zucchini, and potatoes and stir to coat in the oil.

Add the lemon juice and zest, stock, and salt and pepper to taste, cover and cook over medium heat for 20–30 minutes, stirring occasionally.

Remove the lid, sprinkle in the cilantro, and stir well. Serve at once.

vegetable cannelloni

serves 4

10 minutes

45 minutes

1 eggplant
½ cup olive oil
5 cups fresh spinach leaves
2 garlic cloves, crushed
1 tsp ground cumin
2¾ oz/75 g mushrooms, chopped
salt and pepper
12 ready-made cannelloni tubes

tomato sauce

1 tbsp olive oil
1 onion, chopped
2 garlic cloves, crushed
1 lb 12 oz/800 g canned chopped tomatoes
1 tsp superfine sugar
2 tbsp chopped fresh basil
1¾ oz/50 g mozzarella cheese, sliced

This dish is made with prepared cannelloni tubes, but may also be made by rolling ready-bought lasagna sheets.

cook's tip

You can prepare the tomato sauce in advance and store it in the refrigerator for up to 24 hours.

Preheat the oven to 375°F/190°C. Cut the eggplant into small dice.

Heat the oil in a skillet. Add the eggplant and cook for 2–3 minutes.

Add the spinach, garlic, cumin, and mushrooms. Season to taste with salt and pepper and cook for 2–3 minutes, stirring. Spoon the mixture into the cannelloni tubes and arrange in a single layer in an ovenproof dish.

To make the sauce, heat the oil in a pan. Add the onion and garlic and sauté for 1 minute. Add the tomatoes, superfine sugar, and chopped basil and bring to a boil. Lower the heat and let simmer for 5 minutes. Pour the sauce over the cannelloni tubes.

Arrange the sliced mozzarella cheese on top of the sauce and cook in the preheated oven for 30 minutes, or until the cheese is bubbling and golden brown. Serve at once.

cauliflower bake

serves 4

10 minutes

40 minutes

1 lb/450 g cauliflower, broken into florets

2 large potatoes, cubed

3½ oz/100 g cherry tomatoes

sauce

2 tbsp butter or vegetarian margarine

1 leek, sliced

1 garlic clove, crushed

2 tbsp all-purpose flour

1¼ cups milk

scant ¾ cup mixed grated cheese, such as vegetarian Cheddar, Parmesan, and Gruyère

½ tsp paprika

2 tbsp chopped fresh flatleaf parsley, plus extra to garnish

salt and pepper

The red of the tomatoes is a great contrast to the cauliflower and herbs, making this dish appealing to both the eye and the palate.

variation

This dish could be made with broccoli instead of the cauliflower as an alternative.

Preheat the oven to 350°F/180°C. Cook the cauliflower in a pan of boiling water for 10 minutes. Drain well and set aside. Meanwhile, cook the potatoes in a separate pan of boiling water for 10 minutes, drain, and set aside.

To make the sauce, melt the butter in a pan. Add the leek and garlic and sauté for 1 minute. Add the flour and cook for 1 minute. Remove the pan from the heat and gradually stir in the milk, scant ½ cup of the cheese, the paprika, and parsley. Return the pan to the heat and bring to a boil, stirring. Season to taste with salt and pepper.

Spoon the cauliflower into a deep ovenproof dish. Add the cherry tomatoes and top with the potatoes. Pour the sauce over the potatoes and sprinkle on the remaining cheese.

Cook in the preheated oven for 20 minutes, or until the vegetables are cooked through and the cheese is golden brown and bubbling. Garnish with chopped parsley and serve at once.

leek & herb soufflé

serves 4

15 minutes

50 minutes

butter, for greasing
12 oz/350 g baby leeks
1 tbsp olive oil
1/2 cup vegetable stock

scant 1/2 cup walnuts, shelled
2 eggs, separated
2 tbsp chopped fresh mixed herbs
2 tbsp plain yogurt
salt and pepper

Hot soufflés look very impressive if served as soon as they come out of the oven, otherwise they will sink quite quickly.

cook's tip

Placing the soufflé dish on a warmed baking sheet helps to cook the soufflé from the bottom.

Preheat the oven to 350°F/180°C. Grease a 3½-cup soufflé dish and set aside. Using a sharp knife, chop the leeks finely.

Heat the oil in a skillet. Add the leeks and sauté for 2–3 minutes.

Add the stock to the skillet and cook over low heat for 5 minutes.

Place the walnuts in a food processor and process until finely chopped.

Add the leek mixture to the nuts and process to form a purée. Transfer to a large bowl.

Mix the egg yolks, herbs, and yogurt together in a separate bowl and pour into the leek purée. Season to taste with salt and pepper and mix well.

Whisk the egg whites in a clean, dry bowl until stiff peaks form.

Carefully fold the egg whites into the leek mixture, then spoon the mixture into the prepared soufflé dish. Place the dish on a warmed cookie sheet.

Cook in the preheated oven for 35–40 minutes, or until set. Serve the soufflé at once.

artichoke & cheese tart

serves 8

15 minutes

30 minutes

generous 1¼ cups whole-wheat flour, plus extra for dusting

pinch of salt

2 garlic cloves, crushed

2¾ oz/75 g butter or vegetarian margarine

3 tbsp water

filling

2 tbsp olive oil

1 red onion, halved and sliced

10 canned or fresh artichoke hearts

⅞ cup vegetarian Cheddar cheese, grated

1¾ oz/50 g Gorgonzola cheese, crumbled

2 eggs, beaten

1 tbsp chopped fresh rosemary

⅔ cup milk

salt and pepper

Artichoke hearts are delicious to eat, being very delicate in flavor and appearance. They are ideal for cooking in a cheese-flavored pastry shell.

cook's tip

Gently press the center of the tart with your fingertip to test if it is cooked through. It should feel fairly firm, but not solid. If overcooked the flan will start to "weep."

Preheat the oven to 400°F/200°C. To make the pie dough, sift the flour into a large bowl, add the salt, garlic, and butter and rub it in until the mixture resembles bread crumbs. Stir in the water and bring the mixture together to form a dough.

Roll the dough out on a lightly floured counter and use to line an 8-inch/20-cm tart pan. Prick the dough with a fork.

Heat the oil in a skillet. Add the onion and sauté for 3 minutes. Add the artichoke hearts and cook for an additional 2 minutes.

Mix the cheeses, beaten eggs, rosemary, and milk together. Stir in the drained artichoke mixture and season to taste with salt and pepper.

Spoon the artichoke and cheese mixture into the pastry shell and cook in the preheated oven for 25 minutes, or until cooked and set. Serve the tart either hot or cold.

tagliatelle with
zucchini sauce

serves 4

10 minutes

20 minutes

1 lb 7 oz/650 g zucchini
6 tbsp olive oil
3 garlic cloves, crushed
3 tbsp chopped fresh basil
2 fresh red chiles, sliced

juice of 1 large lemon
5 tbsp light cream
4 tbsp freshly grated Parmesan
cheese
salt and pepper
8 oz/225 g dried tagliatelle

This is a fresh tasting dish, which is ideal with a crisp white wine and some crusty bread.

cook's tip

Lime juice and zest could be used instead of the lemon as an alternative.

Using a vegetable peeler, slice the zucchini into thin ribbons.

Heat the oil in a skillet. Add the garlic and sauté for 30 seconds.

Add the zucchini and cook over low heat, stirring, for 5–7 minutes.

Stir in the basil, chiles, lemon juice, cream, and grated Parmesan cheese, then season to taste with salt and pepper.

Meanwhile, cook the pasta in a large pan of lightly salted boiling water for 10 minutes, or until tender but still firm to the bite. Drain the pasta thoroughly and place in a warmed serving bowl.

Pile the zucchini mixture on top of the pasta and serve at once.

olive, bell pepper & cherry tomato pasta

serves 4

10 minutes

25 minutes

8 oz/225 g dried penne
salt and pepper
2 tbsp olive oil
2 tbsp butter
2 garlic cloves, crushed
1 green bell pepper, thinly sliced
1 yellow bell pepper, thinly sliced

16 cherry tomatoes, halved
1 tbsp chopped fresh oregano
½ cup dry white wine
2 tbsp quartered pitted black olives
scant 1¾ cups arugula
fresh oregano sprigs, to garnish

The sweet cherry tomatoes in this recipe add color and flavor and are complemented by the black olives and bell peppers.

Cook the pasta in a large, heavy-bottom pan of boiling salted water for 8–10 minutes, or until tender but still firm to the bite. Drain thoroughly.

Heat the oil and butter in a skillet until the butter melts. Add the garlic and sauté for 30 seconds. Add the bell peppers and cook for 3–4 minutes, stirring constantly.

Stir in the tomatoes, oregano, wine, and olives and cook for 3–4 minutes. Season well with salt and pepper and stir in the arugula until just wilted.

Transfer the pasta to a serving dish, spoon over the sauce, and mix well. Garnish with oregano sprigs and serve.

cook's tip

Ensure that the pan is large enough to prevent the pasta sticking together during cooking.

variation

If arugula is unavailable, fresh spinach makes a good substitute. Follow the same cooking instructions as for arugula.

spinach &
pine nut pasta

 serves 4

 5 minutes

 15 minutes

8 oz/225 g dried pasta shapes
salt and pepper
1/2 cup olive oil
2 garlic cloves, crushed
1 onion, quartered and sliced
3 large flat mushrooms, sliced

5 cups fresh spinach leaves
2 tbsp pine nuts
1/3 cup dry white wine
Parmesan cheese shavings, to garnish

Use any dried pasta shapes that you have for this recipe, the tricolore pasta being the most visually appealing.

cook's tip

To cook perfect pasta, add all the pasta to the boiling water all at once and make sure that the water returns to a boil. Cook, uncovered, until tender but still firm to the bite, then drain thoroughly in a strainer. Transfer to the pan and keep warm until required.

Cook the pasta in a large, heavy-bottom pan of boiling salted water for 8–10 minutes, or until tender but still firm to the bite. Drain well and keep warm until required.

Meanwhile, heat the oil in a large pan. Add the garlic and onion and sauté for 1 minute.

Add the sliced mushrooms and cook for 2 minutes, stirring occasionally.

Add the spinach and cook for 4–5 minutes, or until the spinach is wilted.

Stir in the pine nuts and wine, season well with salt and pepper, and cook for 1 minute.

Transfer the pasta to a warmed serving bowl and toss the sauce into it, mixing well. Garnish with shavings of Parmesan cheese and serve.

tofu & vegetable stir-fry

serves 4

5 minutes

25 minutes

6 oz/175 g potatoes, cubed
1 tbsp olive oil
1 red onion, sliced
8 oz/225 g firm tofu, diced
    (drained weight)
2 zucchini, diced

8 canned artichoke hearts, halved
$\frac{2}{3}$ cup strained tomatoes
1 tsp superfine sugar
2 tbsp chopped fresh basil
salt and pepper

This is a quick dish to prepare, making it ideal as a midweek supper dish, after a busy day at work!

Cook the potatoes in a large pan of boiling water for 10 minutes. Drain thoroughly and set aside until required.

Heat the oil in a large skillet. Add the onion and sauté for 2 minutes, or until the onion has softened.

Stir in the tofu and zucchini and cook for 3–4 minutes, or until they start to brown slightly. Add the potatoes, stirring to mix.

Stir in the artichoke hearts, strained tomatoes, sugar, and basil. Season with salt and pepper and cook for an additional 5 minutes, stirring well. Transfer the stir-fry to serving dishes and serve at once.

cook's tip

Canned artichoke hearts should be drained thoroughly and rinsed before use, because they often have salt added.

variation

Eggplants could be used instead of the zucchini, if preferred.

cantonese garden vegetable stir-fry

serves 4

5 minutes

10 minutes

2 tbsp peanut oil
1 tsp Chinese five-spice powder
2³/4 oz/75 g baby carrots, halved
2 celery stalks, sliced
2 baby leeks, sliced
1³/4 oz/50 g snow peas
4 baby zucchini, halved lengthwise
8 baby corn

8 oz/225 g marinated
   tofu, cubed
4 tbsp fresh orange juice
1 tbsp honey
freshly cooked rice or noodles,
   to serve

to garnish
celery leaves
orange zest

This dish tastes as fresh as it looks. Try to buy baby vegetables because they look and taste so much better in this dish.

Heat the oil in a preheated wok until almost smoking. Add the Chinese five-spice powder, carrots, celery, leeks, snow peas, zucchini, and baby corn and stir-fry for 3–4 minutes.

Add the tofu and cook for an additional 2 minutes, stirring.

Stir in the orange juice and honey, lower the heat, and stir-fry for 1–2 minutes.

Transfer the stir-fry to a serving dish, garnish with celery leaves and orange zest, and serve at once with freshly cooked rice or noodles.

cook's tip

Chinese five-spice powder is a mixture of fennel, star anise, cinnamon bark, cloves, and Szechuan pepper. It is very pungent so should be used sparingly. If kept in an airtight container, it will keep indefinitely.

variation

Lemon juice would be just as delicious as the orange juice in this recipe, but use 3 tablespoons instead of 4 tablespoons.

risotto verde

serves 4

5 minutes

35 minutes

7 cups vegetable stock
2 tbsp olive oil
2 garlic cloves, crushed
2 leeks, shredded
generous 1 cup Arborio rice
1¼ cups dry white wine
4 tbsp chopped fresh mixed herbs

5 cups fresh baby spinach leaves
salt and pepper
3 tbsp plain yogurt
shredded leek, to garnish

Risotto is an Italian dish, which is easy to make and is ideal to serve as an impromptu dinner party meal.

cook's tip

Do not hurry the process of cooking the risotto because the rice must absorb the liquid slowly in order for it to reach the correct consistency.

Pour the stock into a large pan and bring to a boil. Lower the heat to a simmer.

Meanwhile, heat the oil in a separate pan. Add the garlic and leeks and sauté for 2–3 minutes, until softened.

Stir in the rice and cook for 2 minutes, stirring, until well coated.

Pour in half the wine and a little of the hot stock. Cook over low heat until all of the liquid has been absorbed. Add the remaining stock and wine gradually and cook over low heat for 25 minutes, or until the rice is creamy.

Stir in the chopped mixed herbs and baby spinach, season well with salt and pepper, and cook for 2 minutes.

Stir in the yogurt, garnish with the shredded leek, and serve at once.

baked pasta in tomato sauce

serves 8

10 minutes

1 hour 5 minutes

butter, for greasing
3½ oz/100 g dried pasta shapes, such as penne or casareccia
salt and pepper
1 tbsp olive oil
1 leek, chopped
3 garlic cloves, crushed
1 green bell pepper, chopped
14 oz/400 g canned chopped tomatoes

2 tbsp chopped pitted black olives
2 eggs, beaten
1 tbsp chopped fresh basil

tomato sauce
1 tbsp olive oil
1 onion, chopped
8 oz/225 g canned chopped tomatoes
1 tsp superfine sugar
2 tbsp tomato paste
⅔ cup vegetable stock

This pasta dish is baked in an ovenproof bowl and cut into slices for serving. It looks and tastes terrific and is perfect when you want to impress.

Preheat the oven to 350°F/180°C. Grease a 5-cup ovenproof bowl. Cook the pasta in a large, heavy-bottom pan of boiling salted water for 8 minutes. Drain thoroughly.

Meanwhile, heat the oil in a pan. Add the leek and garlic and sauté for 2 minutes, stirring. Add the bell pepper, tomatoes, and olives and cook for an additional 5 minutes.

Remove the pan from the heat and stir in the pasta, beaten eggs, and basil. Season well with salt and pepper, then spoon the mixture into the prepared ovenproof bowl.

Place the ovenproof bowl in a roasting pan and half-fill the pan with boiling water. Cover and cook in the preheated oven for 40 minutes, or until set.

To make the sauce, heat the oil in a pan. Add the onion and sauté for 2 minutes. Add the remaining ingredients, season to taste with salt and pepper, and cook for 10 minutes. Place the sauce in a food processor or blender and process until smooth. Return to a clean pan and reheat gently until hot.

Turn the pasta out of the ovenproof onto a warmed plate. Slice and serve with the tomato sauce.

spaghetti with pear
& walnut sauce

serves 4

10 minutes

20 minutes

8 oz/225 g dried spaghetti

salt and pepper

2 small ripe pears, peeled and sliced

$^2/_3$ cup vegetable stock

$^1/_3$ cup dry white wine

2 tbsp butter

1 tbsp olive oil

1 red onion, quartered and sliced

1 garlic clove, crushed

scant $^1/_2$ cup walnut halves

2 tbsp chopped fresh oregano

1 tbsp lemon juice

2$^3/_4$ oz/75 g Gorgonzola cheese

fresh oregano sprigs, to garnish

*This is quite an unusual
combination of ingredients in a
savory dish, but is absolutely
wonderful tossed into a fine pasta
such as spaghetti.*

cook's tip

*You can use any good-flavored
blue cheese for this dish. Other
varieties to try are Roquefort,
which has a very strong flavor,
Danablu, or Stilton.*

Cook the pasta in a large, heavy-bottom pan of boiling salted water for
8–10 minutes, or until tender but still firm to the bite. Drain thoroughly
and keep warm until required.

Meanwhile, place the pears in a pan and pour over the stock and wine.
Poach the pears over low heat for 10 minutes. Drain and set aside the
cooking liquid and pears.

Heat the butter and oil in a separate pan until the butter melts. Add the
onion and garlic and sauté for 2–3 minutes, stirring constantly.

Add the walnuts, chopped oregano, and lemon juice, stirring.

Stir in the reserved pears with 4 tablespoons of the poaching liquid.

Crumble the Gorgonzola cheese into the pan and cook over low heat,
stirring occasionally, for 1–2 minutes, or until the cheese just starts to melt.
Season to taste with salt and pepper.

Toss the pasta into the sauce, transfer to individual serving plates, and
garnish with oregano sprigs. Serve.

side dishes

If you are running short of ideas for interesting side dishes to serve with your main meals, these recipes will be a welcome inspiration. An ideal accompaniment complements the main dish both visually and nutritionally. Many main dishes will be rich in protein, therefore the side dishes in this chapter have been created to be lighter in texture, but still packed full of color and flavor. They have been cooked in many different ways—there are bakes, steamed vegetables, and braises, all of which are perfect accompaniments for all occasions.

This chapter also contains a selection of delicious salads, which are bursting with flavor and color. Make one of these salads to accompany your meal, or make larger portions to serve alone. The secret of a successful salad relies on one important aspect: the freshness of the ingredients. Try some of the ideas in this chapter and discover some great side dishes to add to your repertoire.

cheese & potato
layer bake

serves 4

20 minutes

I hour 30 minutes

I lb/450 g potatoes

salt and pepper

I leek, sliced

3 garlic cloves, crushed

scant ½ cup vegetarian Cheddar cheese, grated

scant ½ cup mozzarella cheese, grated

¼ cup freshly grated Parmesan cheese

2 tbsp chopped fresh parsley

⅔ cup light cream

⅔ cup milk

chopped fresh flatleaf parsley, to garnish

This is a great side dish, perfect for serving with main meals cooked in the oven.

cook's tip

Stir the vegetables occasionally during the 30 minutes cooking time to prevent them sticking to the bottom of the pan. If the liquid has not evaporated by the end of the cooking time, remove the lid and boil rapidly until the dish is dry.

Preheat the oven to 325°F/160°C. Cook the potatoes in a pan of boiling salted water for 10 minutes. Drain well.

Cut the potatoes into thin slices. Arrange a layer of potatoes in the base of an ovenproof dish. Layer with a little of the leek, garlic, cheeses, and parsley and season well with salt and pepper.

Repeat the layers until all of the ingredients have been used, finishing with a layer of cheese on top.

Mix the cream and milk together, season to taste with salt and pepper, and pour over the potato layers.

Cook in the preheated oven for 1–1¼ hours, or until the cheese is golden brown and bubbling and the potatoes are cooked through.

Garnish with chopped parsley and serve at once.

cauliflower & broccoli
with herb sauce

serves 4

10 minutes

20 minutes

2 baby cauliflowers
8 oz/225 g broccoli
salt and pepper

sauce
8 tbsp olive oil

4 tbsp butter or vegetarian
   margarine
2 tsp grated fresh gingerroot
juice and zest of 2 lemons
5 tbsp chopped fresh cilantro
5 tbsp grated vegetarian Cheddar
   cheese

*Whole baby cauliflowers are
used in this recipe. Try to find
them if you can, if not use large
bunches of florets.*

variation

*Lime or orange could be used
instead of the lemon for a fruity
and refreshing sauce.*

Preheat the broiler to medium. Using a sharp knife, cut the cauliflowers in
half and the broccoli into very large florets.

Cook the cauliflower and broccoli in a pan of boiling salted water for
10 minutes. Drain well, transfer to a shallow ovenproof dish, and keep
warm until required.

To make the sauce, place the oil and butter in a skillet and heat gently until
the butter melts. Add the ginger, lemon juice, lemon zest, and cilantro and
let simmer for 2–3 minutes, stirring occasionally.

Season the sauce with salt and pepper to taste, then pour over the
vegetables in the dish and sprinkle the cheese on top.

Cook under the hot broiler for 2–3 minutes, or until the cheese is
bubbling and golden. Let cool for 1–2 minutes, then serve.

indian spiced potatoes & spinach

serves 4

10 minutes

20–25 minutes

3 tbsp vegetable oil
1 red onion, sliced
2 garlic cloves, crushed
1/2 tsp chili powder
2 tsp ground coriander
1 tsp ground cumin

2/3 cup vegetable stock
10 1/2 oz/300 g potatoes, cubed
1 lb/450 g fresh baby spinach leaves
salt and pepper
1 fresh red chile, sliced

This is a classic Indian accompaniment for curries or plainer main vegetable dishes.

cook's tip

Be very careful when handling chiles—never touch your face or eyes because the juices can be very painful. Always wash your hands thoroughly after preparing chiles. The seeds are the hottest part, but have less flavor, so these are usually removed before use.

Add other vegetables, such as chopped tomatoes, for color and flavor.

Heat the oil in a large skillet. Add the onion and garlic and sauté for 2–3 minutes, stirring occasionally.

Stir in the chili powder, ground coriander, and cumin and cook for an additional 30 seconds.

Add the stock, potatoes, and spinach and bring to a boil. Lower the heat, cover, and let simmer for 10 minutes, or until the potatoes are cooked through.

Season to taste with salt and pepper, add the chile, and cook for an additional 2–3 minutes. Serve at once.

steamed vegetables with vermouth

serves 4

25 minutes

20 minutes

1 carrot, cut into thin sticks
1 fennel bulb, sliced
3 1/2 oz/100 g zucchini, sliced
1 red bell pepper, sliced
4 small onions, halved
8 tbsp vermouth
4 tbsp lime juice

zest of 1 lime
pinch of paprika
salt and pepper
4 fresh tarragon sprigs, plus extra
   to garnish

Serve these vegetables in their paper packages to retain the juices. The result is truly delicious.

cook's tip

Vermouth is a fortified white wine flavored with various herbs and spices. It its available in both sweet and dry forms.

Seal the packages well to prevent them opening during cooking and causing the juices to evaporate.

Place all of the vegetables in a large bowl and mix well.

Cut 4 large squares of parchment paper and place one-quarter of the vegetables in the center of each. Bring the sides of the paper up and pinch together to make an open package.

Mix the vermouth, lime juice, lime zest, and paprika together in a bowl and pour a quarter of the mixture into each package. Season to taste with salt and pepper and add a tarragon sprig to each. Pinch the tops of the packages together to seal.

Place the packages in a steamer, cover, and cook for 15–20 minutes, or until the vegetables are tender. Garnish with tarragon sprigs and serve.

split peas & spinach

serves 4

2 hours 15 minutes

25 minutes

generous 1 cup green split peas
2 lb/900 g fresh spinach leaves
4 tbsp vegetable oil
1 onion, halved and sliced
1 tsp grated fresh gingerroot
1 tsp ground cumin
$^{1}/_{2}$ tsp chili powder

$^{1}/_{2}$ tsp ground coriander
2 garlic cloves, crushed
1$^{1}/_{4}$ cups vegetable stock
salt and pepper

to garnish
fresh cilantro sprigs
lime wedges

This is quite a filling dish, and should be served with a light main course.

Rinse the lentils under cold running water. Transfer to a large bowl, cover with cold water, and let soak for 2 hours. Drain well.

Meanwhile, cook the spinach in a large pan for 5 minutes, or until wilted. Drain well and coarsely chop.

Heat the oil in a large pan. Add the onion, ginger, spices, and garlic and sauté for 2–3 minutes, stirring well. Add the split peas and spinach and stir in the stock. Cover and let simmer for 10–15 minutes, or until the split peas are cooked and the liquid has been absorbed. Season to taste with salt and pepper, garnish with cilantro sprigs and lime wedges, and serve.

cook's tip

Once the split peas have been added, stir occasionally to prevent them sticking to the pan.

variation

If you do not have time to soak the green peas, canned Puy lentils are a good substitute, but remember to drain and rinse them first.

beans in lemon & herb sauce

serves 4

5 minutes

20 minutes

2 lb/900 g mixed green beans, such as fava beans, string beans, or Kentucky wonder beans

2¹/₂ oz/65 g butter or vegetarian margarine

4 tsp all-purpose flour

1¹/₄ cups vegetable stock

¹/₃ cup dry white wine

6 tbsp light cream

3 tbsp chopped fresh mixed herbs

2 tbsp lemon juice

zest of 1 lemon

salt and pepper

Use a variety of beans if possible, although this recipe is perfectly acceptable with just one type of bean.

Cook the beans in a large pan of boiling salted water for 10 minutes, or until tender. Drain and place in a warmed serving dish.

Meanwhile, melt the butter in a pan. Add the flour and cook for 1 minute. Remove the pan from the heat and gradually stir in the stock and wine. Return the pan to the heat and bring to a boil.

Remove the pan from the heat and stir in the light cream, mixed herbs, lemon juice, and zest. Season to taste with salt and pepper. Pour the sauce over the beans, mixing well, and serve at once.

cook's tip

Use a wide range of herbs for flavor, such as rosemary, thyme, tarragon, and sage.

variation

Use lime zest and juice instead of lemon for an alternative citrus flavor. Replace the light cream with plain yogurt for a healthier version of this dish.

 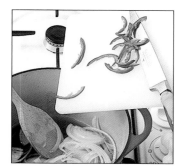 

curried cauliflower & spinach

serves 4

10 minutes

25 minutes

1 cauliflower
6 tbsp vegetable oil
1 tsp mustard seeds
1 tsp ground cumin
1 tsp garam masala
1 tsp ground turmeric
2 garlic cloves, crushed

1 onion, halved and sliced
1 fresh green chile, sliced
1 lb/450 g fresh spinach leaves
1/3 cup vegetable stock
1 tbsp chopped fresh cilantro
salt and pepper
fresh cilantro sprigs, to garnish

The contrast in color in this recipe makes it very appealing to the eye, especially as the cauliflower is lightly colored with turmeric.

Break the cauliflower into small florets.

Heat the oil in a deep ovenproof casserole. Add the mustard seeds and cook until they start to pop.

Stir in the remaining spices, the garlic, onion, and chile and cook for 2–3 minutes, stirring.

Add the cauliflower, spinach, stock, and cilantro, then season to taste with salt and pepper and cook, covered, over low heat for 15 minutes, or until the cauliflower is tender. Uncover the dish and boil for 1 minute to thicken the juices. Garnish with cilantro sprigs and serve.

cook's tip

Mustard seeds are used throughout India and are particularly popular in vegetarian cooking in the south. They are sautéed in oil first to bring out their flavor before the other ingredients are added.

variation

Broccoli may be used instead of the cauliflower, if preferred.

eggplant & zucchini galette

serves 4

40 minutes

1 hour 15 minutes

2 large eggplants, sliced

salt and pepper

4 zucchini

1 lb 12 oz/800 g canned chopped
   tomatoes, drained

2 tbsp tomato paste

2 garlic cloves, crushed

1/4 cup olive oil, plus extra
   for cooking

1 tsp superfine sugar

2 tbsp chopped fresh basil

8 oz/225 g mozzarella cheese, sliced

fresh basil leaves, to garnish

This is a dish of eggplant and zucchini layered with a quick tomato sauce and melted cheese.

Place the eggplant slices in a strainer and sprinkle with salt. Let stand for 30 minutes, then rinse well under cold running water and drain. Thinly slice the zucchini.

Meanwhile, preheat the oven to 350°F/180°C. Place the tomatoes, tomato paste, garlic, oil, sugar, and chopped basil in a pan and let simmer for 20 minutes, or until reduced by half. Season well with salt and pepper.

Heat 2 tablespoons of oil in a large skillet. Add the eggplant slices and cook for 2–3 minutes, until just starting to brown. Remove the eggplant slices from the skillet.

Add an additional 2 tablespoons of oil to the skillet and cook the zucchini slices until browned.

Arrange half of the eggplant slices in the base of an ovenproof dish. Top with half of the tomato sauce and the zucchini slices and then half of the mozzarella cheese.

Repeat the layers and bake in the preheated oven for 45–50 minutes, or until the vegetables are tender. Garnish with basil leaves and serve.

baked celery with
cream & pecans

serves 4

15 minutes

40 minutes

I head of celery
1/2 tsp ground cumin
1/2 tsp ground coriander
I garlic clove, crushed
I red onion, thinly sliced
scant 1/2 cup pecan halves
2/3 cup vegetable stock

2/3 cup light cream
salt and pepper
7/8 cup fresh whole-wheat
   bread crumbs
1/4 cup freshly grated Parmesan
   cheese
celery leaves, to garnish

This dish is topped with bread crumbs for a crunchy topping, which is hiding a creamy celery and pecan mixture.

Preheat the oven to 400°F/200°C. Trim the celery and cut into short thin sticks. Place the celery in an ovenproof dish with the ground cumin, coriander, garlic, onion, and pecans.

Mix the stock and cream together in a measuring cup or pitcher and pour over the vegetables. Season to taste with salt and pepper.

Mix the bread crumbs and cheese together and sprinkle over the top to cover the vegetables.

Cook in the preheated oven for 40 minutes, or until the vegetables are tender and the top crispy. Garnish with celery leaves and serve.

cook's tip

Once grated, Parmesan cheese quickly loses its "bite" so it is best to grate only the amount you need for the recipe. Wrap the rest tightly in foil and it will keep for several months in the refrigerator.

variation

You could use carrots or zucchini instead of the celery, if you prefer.

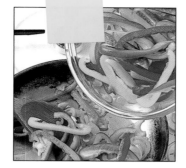

pepperonata

serves 4

15 minutes

40 minutes

4 tbsp olive oil
1 onion, halved and finely sliced
2 red bell peppers, cut into strips
2 green bell peppers, cut into strips
2 yellow bell peppers, cut into strips
2 garlic cloves, crushed

1 lb 12 oz/800 g canned chopped tomatoes, drained
2 tbsp chopped fresh cilantro
salt and pepper
2 tbsp chopped pitted black olives

A delicious mixture of bell peppers and onions, cooked with tomatoes and herbs for a rich side dish.

Heat the oil in a large skillet. Add the onion and sauté for 5 minutes, stirring until just starting to colour.

Add the bell peppers and garlic to the skillet and cook for an additional 3–4 minutes.

Stir in the tomatoes and cilantro and season to taste with salt and pepper. Cover and cook the vegetables gently for 30 minutes, or until the mixture is dry.

Stir in the pitted black olives and serve at once.

cook's tip

Stir the vegetables occasionally during the 30 minutes cooking time to prevent them sticking to the bottom of the skillet. If the liquid has not evaporated by the end of the cooking time, remove the lid, and boil rapidly until the dish is dry.

variation

If you don't like the distinctive flavor of fresh cilantro, you can substitute it with 2 tablespoons chopped fresh flatleaf parsley. Use green olives instead of black ones, if you prefer.

souffléd cheesy potato fries

serves 4	
20 minutes	
25 minutes	

2 lb/900 g potatoes, cut into chunks
salt and pepper
2/3 cup heavy cream
scant 3/4 cup Gruyère cheese, grated
pinch of cayenne pepper

2 egg whites
vegetable oil, for deep-frying

to garnish

chopped fresh flatleaf parsley
grated vegetarian Cheddar cheese

These small potato chunks are mixed in a creamy cheese sauce and cooked in oil until deliciously golden brown.

Cook the potatoes in a pan of boiling salted water for 10 minutes. Drain well and pat dry with paper towels. Set aside until required.

Mix the heavy cream and Gruyère cheese together in a large bowl. Stir in the cayenne and season to taste with salt and pepper.

Whisk the egg whites in a clean, dry bowl until stiff peaks form. Fold into the cheese mixture until fully incorporated.

Add the cooked potatoes, turning to coat thoroughly in the mixture.

Heat the oil for deep-frying in a heavy-bottom pan to 350°F/180°C, or until a cube of bread browns in 30 seconds. Remove the potatoes from the cheese mixture with a slotted spoon and cook in the oil, in batches, for 3–4 minutes, or until golden.

Transfer the potatoes to a serving dish and garnish with parsley and grated cheese. Serve.

variation

Add other flavorings, such as grated nutmeg or curry powder, to the cream and cheese.

bulgur pilau

serves 4

15 minutes

35–40 minutes

2³⁄₄ oz/75 g butter or vegetarian margarine

1 red onion, halved and sliced

2 garlic cloves, crushed

2 cups bulgur wheat

6 oz/175 g tomatoes, seeded and chopped

1³⁄₄ oz/50 g baby corn, halved lengthwise

2³⁄₄ oz/75 g small broccoli florets

3¹⁄₂ cups vegetable stock

2 tbsp honey

generous ¹⁄₄ cup golden raisins

scant ¹⁄₂ cup pine nuts

¹⁄₂ tsp ground cinnamon

¹⁄₂ tsp ground cumin

salt and pepper

sliced scallions, to garnish

Bulgur wheat is very easy to use and is a delicious alternative to rice, having a distinctive nutty flavor.

cook's tip

The dish is left to stand for 10 minutes in order for the bulgur to finish cooking and to let the flavors mingle.

Melt the butter in a large ovenproof casserole.

Add the onion and garlic and sauté for 2–3 minutes, stirring occasionally.

Add the bulgur wheat, tomatoes, baby corn, broccoli, and stock and bring to a boil. Lower the heat, cover, and cook for 15–20 minutes, stirring occasionally.

Stir in the honey, golden raisins, pine·nuts, ground cinnamon, cumin, and salt and pepper to taste. Mix well, then remove the casserole from the heat, cover, and let stand for 10 minutes.

Spoon the bulgur pilau into a warmed serving dish.

Garnish with sliced scallions and serve at once.

pesto potatoes

serves 4

15 minutes

15 minutes

2 lb/900 g small new potatoes
salt and pepper·
2¾ oz/75 g fresh basil
2 tbsp pine nuts
3 garlic cloves, crushed

generous ⅓ cup olive oil
scant ¾ cup freshly grated
    Parmesan cheese and romano
    cheese, mixed
fresh basil sprigs, to garnish

*Pesto sauce is more commonly
used as a pasta sauce,
but is delicious served over
potatoes as well.*

cook's tip

*Store this pesto sauce in an airtight
container for up to 1 week in the
refrigerator. It can also be frozen
(before adding the cheeses)
for several months.*

*This sauce would also make
a great dressing for a
crisp green salad.*

Cook the potatoes in a pan of boiling salted water for 15 minutes, or until tender. Drain well, transfer to a warmed serving dish, and keep warm until required.

Meanwhile, place the basil, pine nuts, garlic, and a little salt and pepper to taste in a food processor and process for 30 seconds, adding the oil gradually, until smooth.

Transfer the mixture to a large bowl and stir in the grated Parmesan and romano cheeses.

Spoon the pesto sauce over the potatoes and mix well. Garnish with fresh basil sprigs and serve at once.

carrot, orange & poppy seed bake

serves 4

20 minutes

40 minutes

1 lb 8 oz/675 g carrots, cut into thin strips
1 leek, sliced
salt and pepper
1¼ cups fresh orange juice
2 tbsp honey
1 garlic clove, crushed
1 tsp ground allspice
2 tsp chopped fresh thyme
1 tbsp poppy seeds

to garnish
fresh thyme sprigs
orange zest

The poppy seeds add texture and flavor to this recipe, and also counteract the slightly sweet flavor of the carrots.

Preheat the oven to 350°F/180°C. Cook the carrots and leek in a pan of boiling salted water for 5–6 minutes. Drain well and transfer to a shallow baking dish. Set aside until required.

Mix the orange juice, honey, garlic, allspice, and thyme together and pour the mixture over the vegetables. Add salt and pepper to taste.

Cover and cook in the preheated oven for 30 minutes, or until the vegetables are tender. Uncover and sprinkle with poppy seeds. Garnish with fresh thyme sprigs and orange zest and serve.

cook's tip

Lemon or lime juice could be used instead of the orange juice, if you prefer. Garnish with lemon or lime zest.

variation

If you prefer, use 2 teaspoons ground cumin instead of the allspice and omit the thyme. Cumin works particularly well with carrots.

greek beans

serves 4

5 minutes

1 hour 5 minutes

14 oz/400 g canned Great Northern
  beans, drained and rinsed
1 tbsp olive oil
3 garlic cloves, crushed
scant 2 cups vegetable stock
1 bay leaf

2 fresh oregano sprigs
1 tbsp tomato paste
juice of 1 lemon
1 small red onion, chopped
2 tbsp pitted black olives, halved
salt and pepper

*This dish contains many Greek
flavors such as lemon, garlic,
oregano, and olives, for a
really flavorful recipe.*

Place the Great Northern beans in an ovenproof casserole.

Add the oil and crushed garlic and cook over low heat, stirring
occasionally, for 4–5 minutes.

Add the stock, bay leaf, oregano, tomato paste, lemon juice, and onion,
then cover and let simmer for 1 hour, or until the sauce has thickened.

Stir in the olives, season to taste with salt and pepper, and serve.

cook's tip

*This dish may be made in
advance and served cold with
crusty bread, if preferred.*

variation

*You can substitute other canned
beans for the Great Northern
beans—try cannellini, black-eye
peas, or chickpeas instead. Drain
and rinse them thoroughly before
use because canned beans often
have sugar or salt added.*

sweet & sour eggplants

serves 4

45 minutes

30 minutes

2 large eggplants
salt and pepper
6 tbsp olive oil
4 garlic cloves, crushed
1 onion, cut into 8 wedges
4 large tomatoes, seeded
 and chopped

3 tbsp chopped fresh mint
2/3 cup vegetable stock
4 tsp brown sugar
2 tbsp red wine vinegar
1 tsp red pepper flakes
fresh mint sprigs, to garnish

This is a dish of Persian origin, not Chinese as it sounds. Eggplants are cooked and mixed with tomatoes, mint, sugar, and vinegar for a really intense flavor.

cook's tip

Mint is a popular herb in Middle Eastern cooking. It is a useful herb to grow because it can be added to a variety of dishes, particularly salads and vegetable dishes. It can be grown easily in a garden or window box.

Using a sharp knife, cut the eggplants into cubes. Place them in a strainer, sprinkle with salt, and let stand for 30 minutes. Rinse thoroughly under cold running water and drain well. This process removes all the bitter juices from the eggplants. Pat dry with paper towels.

Heat the oil in a skillet. Add the eggplant and sauté, stirring constantly, for 1–2 minutes.

Stir in the garlic and onion and cook for an additional 2–3 minutes.

Stir in the tomatoes, mint, and stock, cover, and cook for 15–20 minutes, or until the vegetables are tender.

Stir in the sugar, red wine vinegar, and red pepper flakes, season to taste with salt and pepper, and cook for 2–3 minutes. Transfer the eggplant to serving plates, garnish with mint sprigs, and serve.

mini vegetable puff pastry shells

serves 4

15 minutes

35 minutes

1 lb/450 g ready-made puff pastry
all-purpose flour, for dusting
1 egg, beaten

filling
8 oz/225 g sweet potato, cubed
3½ oz/100 g baby asparagus spears

2 tbsp butter or vegetarian
   margarine
1 leek, sliced
2 small open-cap mushrooms, sliced
1 tsp lime juice
1 tsp chopped fresh thyme
pinch of dried mustard
salt and pepper

These are ideal with a more formal meal as they take a little time to prepare and look impressive.

cook's tip

Use a colorful selection of any vegetables you have at hand for this recipe.

Preheat the oven to 400°F/200°C. Cut the puff pastry into 4 equal-size pieces. Roll each piece out on a lightly floured counter to form a 5-inch/13-cm square. Place on a dampened baking sheet and score a smaller 3-inch/7.5-cm square inside.

Brush with beaten egg and cook in the preheated oven for 20 minutes, or until risen and golden brown.

Remove the pastry squares from the oven and carefully cut out the central square of pastry, then lift out and set aside.

To make the filling, cook the sweet potato in a pan of boiling water for 15 minutes, then drain well. Blanch the asparagus in a separate pan of boiling water for 10 minutes, or until tender. Drain and set aside until required.

Melt the butter in another pan. Add the leek and mushrooms and sauté for 2–3 minutes. Add the lime juice, thyme, and mustard, season well with salt and pepper, and stir in the sweet potatoes and asparagus. Spoon into the pastry shells, top with the reserved pastry squares, and serve.

eggplant salad

serves 4

1 hour 10 minutes

10–15 minutes

1 large eggplant
salt and pepper
vegetable oil, for oiling
3 tbsp sesame seed paste
juice and zest of 1 lemon
1 garlic clove, crushed
pinch of paprika

1 tbsp chopped fresh cilantro
Boston lettuce leaves

to garnish
strips of pimiento
lemon wedges
toasted sesame seeds

This salad uses sesame seed paste as a flavoring for the dressing, which complements the eggplant.

cook's tip

Sesame seed paste is a nutty-flavored sauce made from ground sesame seeds and is available from most health foodstores. It is good served with Middle Eastern dishes.

Using a sharp knife, cut the eggplant in half, place in a strainer, and sprinkle with salt. Let stand for 30 minutes, then rinse under cold running water and drain well. Pat dry with paper towels. Meanwhile, preheat the oven to 450°F/230°C.

Place the eggplant halves, skin-side uppermost, on an oiled baking sheet and cook in the preheated oven for 10–15 minutes. Remove from the oven and let cool.

Cut the eggplant into cubes and set aside until required. Mix the sesame seed paste, lemon juice and zest, garlic, paprika, and cilantro together in a bowl. Season to taste with salt and pepper and stir in the eggplant.

Line a serving plate with lettuce leaves and spoon the eggplant into the center. Garnish the salad with pimiento strips, lemon wedges, and toasted sesame seeds and serve.

salad with garlic &
yogurt dressing

serves 4

20 minutes

–

2¾ oz/75 g cucumber,
  cut into sticks

6 scallions, halved

2 tomatoes, seeded
  and cut into 8 pieces

1 yellow bell pepper, cut into strips

2 celery stalks, cut into strips

4 radishes, quartered

2¾ oz/75 g corn salad

1 tbsp chopped fresh mint, to serve

dressing

2 tbsp lemon juice

1 garlic clove, crushed

⅔ cup plain yogurt

2 tbsp olive oil

salt and pepper

This is a very quick and refreshing salad using a whole range of colorful ingredients, which make it look as good as it tastes.

cook's tip

If corn salad is unavailable, then use the same amount of arugula instead.

Do not toss the dressing into the salad until just before serving, otherwise it will turn soggy.

Mix the cucumber, scallions, tomatoes, bell pepper, celery, radishes, and corn salad together in a large serving bowl.

To make the dressing, stir the lemon juice, garlic, yogurt, and oil together. Season well with salt and pepper.

Spoon the dressing over the salad and toss to mix.

Sprinkle the salad with chopped mint and serve.

zucchini, yogurt
& mint salad

serves 4

10–15 minutes

10 minutes

2 zucchini, cut into sticks
3½ oz/100 g green beans,
   cut into 3 pieces
salt
1 green bell pepper, cut into strips
2 celery stalks, sliced
1 bunch of watercress

dressing
scant 1 cup plain yogurt
1 garlic clove, crushed
2 tbsp chopped fresh mint
pepper

This salad uses lots of green-colored ingredients, which look and taste wonderful with the minty yogurt dressing.

cook's tip

The salad must be served as soon as the yogurt dressing has been added—the dressing will start to separate if kept for any length of time.

Watercress is available all year round. Its fresh peppery flavor makes it a delicious addition to many salads.

Cook the zucchini and green beans in a pan of boiling salted water for 7–8 minutes. Drain and let cool completely.

Mix the zucchini and green beans with the bell pepper, celery, and watercress in a large bowl.

To make the dressing, mix the yogurt, garlic, and chopped mint together in a bowl. Season with pepper to taste.

Spoon the dressing over the salad and serve at once.

bean, avocado &
tomato salad

serves 4

10–15 minutes

–

red leaf lettuce
2 ripe avocados
2 tsp lemon juice
4 tomatoes
1 onion
6 oz/175 g mixed canned beans, drained

dressing
4 tbsp olive oil
drop of chili oil
2 tbsp garlic wine vinegar
pinch of superfine sugar
pinch of chili powder
1 tbsp chopped fresh parsley

This is a colorful salad with a Mexican theme, using beans, tomatoes, and avocado. The chili dressing adds a little kick.

cook's tip

The lemon juice is sprinkled onto the avocados to prevent discoloration when in contact with the air. For this reason the salad should be prepared, assembled, and served quite quickly.

Instead of whisking the dressing, place all the ingredients in a screw-top jar and shake vigorously. Any leftover dressing can be stored in the same jar.

Line a serving bowl with the lettuce.

Using a sharp knife, thinly slice the avocados and sprinkle with the lemon juice. Thinly slice the tomato and onion.

Arrange the avocado, tomatoes, and onion round the salad bowl, leaving a space in the center.

Spoon the beans into the center of the salad. Place all the ingredients for the dressing in a bowl and whisk together. Pour the dressing over the salad and serve at once.

gado gado

serves 4

10 minutes

25 minutes

3¹/₂ oz/100 g white cabbage, shredded

3¹/₂ oz/100 g green beans, cut into 3 pieces

3¹/₂ oz/100 g carrots, cut into short thin sticks

3¹/₂ oz/100 g cauliflower florets

²/₃ cup bean sprouts

salt

dressing

generous ¹/₃ cup vegetable oil

generous ⁵/₈ cup unsalted peanuts

2 garlic cloves, crushed

1 small onion, finely chopped

¹/₂ tsp chili powder

¹/₃ tsp light brown sugar

scant 2 cups water

juice of ¹/₂ lemon

sliced scallions, to garnish

This is a very well-known Indonesian salad of mixed vegetables with a peanut dressing.

cook's tip

If necessary, you can prepare the peanut dressing in advance and store it in the refrigerator for up to 12 hours before serving.

Cook the vegetables separately in a pan of boiling salted water for 4–5 minutes, drain well, and let chill in the refrigerator.

To make the dressing, heat the oil in a skillet. Add the peanuts and cook for 3–4 minutes, turning.

Remove from the skillet with a slotted spoon and let drain on paper towels. Grind the peanuts in a blender or crush with a rolling pin until a fine mixture is formed.

Pour all but 1 tablespoon oil from the skillet. Add the garlic and onion and sauté for 1 minute. Add the chili powder, sugar, a pinch of salt, and the water and bring to a boil.

Stir in the peanuts. Lower the heat and let simmer for 4–5 minutes, until the sauce thickens. Add the lemon juice and let cool.

Arrange the vegetables in a serving dish and spoon the peanut dressing into the center. Garnish with sliced scallions and serve.

broiled vegetable
salad with mustard dressing

serves 4

1 hour 15 minutes

10 minutes

1 zucchini, sliced
1 yellow bell pepper, sliced
1 eggplant, sliced
1 fennel bulb, cut into 8 pieces
1 red onion, cut into 8 wedges
16 cherry tomatoes
3 tbsp olive oil
1 garlic clove, crushed
fresh rosemary sprigs, to garnish

dressing
4 tbsp olive oil
2 tbsp balsamic vinegar
2 tsp chopped fresh rosemary
1 tsp Dijon mustard
1 tsp honey
2 tsp lemon juice

The vegetables for this dish are best prepared well in advance and chilled before serving.

cook's tip

This dish could also be served warm—heat the dressing in a pan and toss into the vegetables.

Preheat the broiler to medium. Place all of the vegetables except for the cherry tomatoes onto a baking sheet.

Mix the oil and garlic and brush over the vegetables. Cook under the hot broiler for 10 minutes, until tender and starting to char. Let cool. Spoon the vegetables and the cherry tomatoes into a serving bowl.

Mix all the ingredients for the dressing together in a bowl, then pour over the vegetables. Cover and let chill in the refrigerator for 1 hour. Garnish with rosemary sprigs and serve.

red cabbage &
pear salad

serves 4

15 minutes

–

12 oz/350 g red cabbage,
finely shredded

2 Bartlett pears,
thinly sliced

4 scallions, sliced

leaf lettuce

1 carrot, grated

fresh chives, to garnish

dressing

4 tbsp pear juice

1 tsp whole-grain mustard

3 tbsp olive oil

1 tbsp garlic wine vinegar

1 tbsp snipped fresh chives

*Red cabbage is much underused—
it is a colorful and tasty ingredient,
which is perfect with fruits, such
as pears or apples.*

Toss the cabbage, pears, and scallions together in a bowl.

Line a serving dish with lettuce leaves and spoon the cabbage and pear mixture into the center. Sprinkle the carrot into the center of the cabbage to form a domed pile.

To make the dressing, mix the pear juice, mustard, oil, vinegar, and snipped chives together in a bowl.

Pour the dressing over the salad, garnish with chives, and serve.

cook's tip

*Mix the salad just before serving
to prevent the color from the red
cabbage bleeding into the
other ingredients.*

variation

*Experiment with different types
of salad greens. The slightly bitter
flavor of chicory or radicchio
would work well with the
sweetness of the pears.*

alfalfa, beet & spinach salad

serves 4

10 minutes

–

generous 2 cups fresh baby
  spinach leaves
2¾ oz/75 g alfalfa sprouts
2 celery stalks, sliced
4 cooked beet, cut into 8 wedges

dressing

4 tbsp olive oil
1½ tbsp garlic wine vinegar
1 garlic clove, crushed
2 tsp honey
1 tbsp snipped fresh chives

*This is a refreshing salad
that must be assembled just
before serving to prevent all of the
ingredients being tainted pink
by the beet.*

Place the spinach and alfalfa sprouts in a large bowl and mix together.

Add the celery and mix well.

Toss in the beet and mix well.

To make the dressing, mix the oil, wine vinegar, garlic, honey, and snipped chives together in a bowl.

Pour the dressing over the salad, toss well, and serve at once.

cook's tip

*If the spinach leaves are too
large, tear them up rather than
cutting them because cutting
bruises the leaves.*

*Alfalfa sprouts should be available
from most supermarkets, if not,
use bean sprouts instead.*

variation

*Add the segments of 1 large orange
to the salad to make it even more
colorful and refreshing. Replace the
garlic wine vinegar with a different
flavored oil, such as chili or herb, if
you prefer.*

desserts

Vegetarian or not, confirmed dessert lovers feel a meal is lacking if there isn't a tempting dessert to finish off with. Desserts help to satisfy a deep-seated desire for something sweet and they make us feel good. However, they are often loaded with fat and sugar. Some of the recipes in this chapter offer the perfect solution—they are light, but full of flavor, so you can still enjoy that sweet treat without the bulging waistline!

This chapter contains a wonderful selection of irresistible desserts, perfect for rounding off a meal. There are simple fruit fools that are quick to make, cakes, exotic fruit tarts, and all time favorites, such as a chocolate cheesecake and steamed sponges. As mentioned in the introduction, vegetarian alternatives may be used for cream and milk in the recipes, and vegetarian gelatine has been used in those recipes that require setting. So take your pick and dip into a delicious dessert!

raspberry fool

serves 4

1 hour 15 minutes

–

generous 1 1/4 cups fresh raspberries
scant 1/2 cup confectioners' sugar
1 1/4 cups sour cream
1/2 tsp vanilla extract
2 egg whites

to decorate

fresh raspberries
lemon balm leaves

This dish is very easy to make and can be made in advance and stored in the refrigerator.

Place the raspberries and confectioners' sugar in a food processor or blender and process until smooth.

Set aside 1 tablespoon per portion of sour cream for decorating.

Place the vanilla extract and sour cream in a bowl and stir in the raspberry mixture.

Whisk the egg whites in a separate clean, dry bowl until stiff peaks form. Using a metal spoon, fold the egg whites into the raspberry mixture until fully incorporated.

Spoon the raspberry fool into serving dishes and let chill in the refrigerator for at least 1 hour. Decorate with the reserved sour cream, raspberries, and lemon balm leaves and serve.

cook's tip

Although this dessert is best made with fresh raspberries in season, an acceptable result can be achieved with frozen raspberries, which are available from most supermarkets.

Sour cream often contains extra ingredients, such as gelatin, so remember to read the label first.

variation

This recipe is also delicious made with strawberries or blackberries.

chocolate mousse

serves 8

2 hours 15 minutes

5 minutes

3 1/2 oz/100 g semisweet chocolate, melted

1 1/4 cups plain yogurt

2/3 cup Quark

4 tbsp superfine sugar

1 tbsp orange juice

1 tbsp brandy

1 1/2 tsp vegetarian gelatin

9 tbsp cold water

2 large egg whites

to decorate

coarsely grated semisweet chocolate

coarsely grated white chocolate

orange zest

This is a light and fluffy, but fruity-tasting mousse, which is delicious with a fresh fruit sauce.

cook's tip

For a quick fruit sauce, blend a can of mandarin segments in natural juice in a food processor and press through a strainer. Stir in 1 tablespoon honey and serve with the mousse.

Place the melted chocolate, yogurt, Quark, superfine sugar, orange juice, and brandy in a food processor and process for 30 seconds. Transfer the mixture to a large bowl.

Sprinkle the vegetarian gelatin over the cold water and stir until dissolved.

Place the vegetarian gelatin and water in a small pan and bring to a boil for 2 minutes. Let cool slightly, then stir into the chocolate mixture.

Whisk the egg whites in a clean, dry bowl until stiff peaks form, then, using a metal spoon, fold into the chocolate mixture.

Line a 3½-cup loaf pan with plastic wrap. Spoon the mousse into the pan and let chill in the refrigerator for 2 hours, until set. Turn the mousse out onto a serving plate, decorate with coarsely grated semisweet and white chocolate, and orange zest and serve.

berry cheesecake

serves 8

2 hours 15 minutes

5 minutes

base
2¾ oz/75 g vegetarian margarine
6 oz/175 g oatmeal cookies
scant ½ cup dry unsweetened
coconut

topping
⅔ cup cold water
1½ tsp vegetarian gelatin

½ cup evaporated milk
1 egg
6 tbsp light brown sugar
1 lb/450 g soft cream cheese
1½ cups mixed berries
2 tbsp honey

Use a mixture of berries, such as blueberries, blackberries, raspberries, and strawberries, for a really fruity cheesecake.

Line the base of an 8-inch/20-cm springform cake pan. Place the margarine in a pan and heat until melted. Place the cookies in a food processor and process until smooth. Alternatively, place in a plastic bag and crush with a rolling pin. Stir into the melted margarine with the coconut.

Press the mixture into the prepared springform pan and let chill in the refrigerator while preparing the filling.

To make the topping, place the water in a small pan and sprinkle the vegetarian gelatin over. Stir to dissolve, then bring to a boil and boil for 2 minutes. Remove the pan from the heat and let cool slightly.

Place the evaporated milk, egg, sugar, and soft cream cheese in a bowl and beat until smooth. Stir in scant ¼ cup of the berries. Stir in the vegetarian gelatin in a stream, stirring constantly, until fully incorporated.

cook's tip

Warm the honey slightly to make it runnier and easier to drizzle.

Spoon the mixture onto the cookie base and return to the refrigerator for 2 hours, or until set.

Remove the cheesecake from the pan and transfer to a serving plate. Arrange the remaining berries on top of the cheesecake and drizzle the honey over the top. Serve.

steamed coffee sponge & sauce

serves 4

10 minutes

1 hour 15 minutes

2 tbsp vegetarian margarine, plus extra for greasing
2 tbsp soft brown sugar
2 eggs
scant 1/3 cup all-purpose flour
3/4 tsp baking powder
6 tbsp milk
1 tsp coffee flavoring

sauce
1 1/4 cups milk
1 tbsp soft brown sugar
1 tsp unsweetened cocoa
2 tbsp cornstarch
4 tbsp cold water

This sponge pudding is very light and is delicious with a coffee or chocolate sauce.

Lightly grease a 2 1/2-cup ovenproof bowl. Place the margarine and sugar in a bowl and cream together until light and fluffy. Beat in the eggs.

Gradually stir in the flour and baking powder, then stir in the milk and coffee flavoring to form a smooth batter.

Spoon the mixture into the prepared ovenproof bowl and cover with a pleated piece of parchment paper and a pleated piece of foil, securing round the bowl with string. Place in a steamer or large pan and half-fill with boiling water. Cover and steam for 1–1 1/4 hours, or until cooked through.

To make the sauce, place the milk, soft brown sugar, and unsweetened cocoa in a pan and heat until the sugar dissolves. Blend the cornstarch with the cold water to form a paste, then stir into the pan. Bring to a boil, stirring, until thickened. Cook over low heat for 1 minute.

Turn the pudding out onto a serving plate and spoon the sauce over the top. Serve.

cook's tip

The pudding is covered with pleated paper and foil to allow it to rise. The foil will react with the steam and must not be placed directly against the pudding.

fruit brûlée

serves 4

1 hour 15 minutes

15 minutes

4 plums, pitted and sliced
2 cooking apples, peeled and sliced
2 tbsp water
1 tsp ground ginger
2¹/2 cups strained plain yogurt

2 tbsp confectioners' sugar, sifted
1 tsp almond extract
scant ¹/2 cup raw brown sugar

This is a cheat's brûlée, in that yogurt is used to cover a base of fruit, before being sprinkled with sugar and broiled.

Place the plums and apples in a pan with the water and cook for 7–10 minutes, or until tender but not mushy. Remove the pan from the heat, let cool, then stir in the ginger.

Preheat the broiler to medium. Using a slotted spoon, spoon the mixture into the base of a shallow serving dish.

Mix the strained plain yogurt, confectioners' sugar, and almond extract together in a bowl and spoon onto the fruit to cover the fruit completely.

Sprinkle the raw brown sugar over the top of the yogurt and cook under the hot broiler for 3–4 minutes, or until the sugar has dissolved and formed a crust. Let chill in the refrigerator for 1 hour, then serve.

cook's tip

Use any variety of fruit, such as mixed berries or mango pieces, for this dessert, but do not poach them.

variation

You can vary the fruit in this dish, depending on what is in season—try fresh apricots or peaches. Alternatively, use 14 oz/400 g canned fruit cocktail.

pear cake

serves 12

25 minutes

1 hour 30 minutes

vegetarian margarine, for greasing
4 pears, peeled and cored
2 tbsp water
generous 1 1/4 cups all-purpose flour
2 tsp baking powder
1/2 cup light brown sugar

4 tbsp milk
2 tbsp honey, plus extra
   for drizzling
2 tsp ground cinnamon
2 egg whites

This is a really moist cake, flavored with chopped pears and cinnamon.

Preheat the oven to 300°F/150°C. Grease and line the base of an 8-inch/20-cm cake pan.

Place 1 pear in a food processor with the water and process until almost smooth. Transfer to a large bowl.

Sift in the all-purpose flour and baking powder, then beat in the sugar, milk, honey, and cinnamon and mix well with your fingers.

Chop 2 of the remaining pears and add to the mixture.

Whisk the egg whites in a clean, dry bowl until peaks form, then gently fold into the mixture until fully incorporated.

Slice the remaining pear and arrange in a fan pattern on the base of the prepared pan.

Spoon the cake batter into the pan and cook in the preheated oven for 1 1/4 – 1 1/2 hours, or until cooked through. Remove the cake from the oven and let cool in the pan for 10 minutes.

Turn the cake out onto a wire rack and drizzle with honey. Let cool completely, then cut into slices to serve.

cook's tip

To test if the cake is cooked through, insert a skewer into the center—if it comes out clean the cake is cooked. If not, return the cake to the oven and test at frequent intervals.

fruit & nut loaf

makes I loaf

I hour 35 minutes

40 minutes

1 1/2 cups strong white bread flour, plus extra for dusting

1/2 tsp salt

1 tbsp vegetarian margarine, plus extra for greasing

2 tbsp light brown sugar

generous 1/2 cup golden raisins

generous 1/4 cup no-soak dried apricots, chopped

generous 1/4 cup chopped hazelnuts

2 tsp active dry yeast

6 tbsp orange juice

6 tbsp plain yogurt

2 tbsp strained apricot jelly

This loaf is like a fruit bread, which may be served warm or cold, perhaps spread with a little vegetarian margarine or butter or topped with jelly.

Sift the flour and salt into a large bowl. Rub in the margarine, then stir in the sugar, golden raisins, apricots, nuts, and yeast.

Warm the orange juice in a pan, but do not let boil.

Stir the warmed orange juice into the flour mixture with the yogurt and bring the mixture together to form a dough.

Knead the dough on a lightly floured counter for 5 minutes, until smooth and elastic. Form into a circle and place on a lightly greased baking sheet. Cover with a clean dish towel and let rise in a warm place until doubled in size.

Preheat the oven to 425°F/220°C. Cook the loaf in the oven for 35–40 minutes, or until cooked through. Transfer to a wire rack and brush with the apricot jelly. Let cool before serving.

cook's tip

To test if the loaf is cooked through, tap the base—if it sounds hollow, it's cooked.

variation

You can vary the nuts according to whatever you have at hand—try chopped walnuts or almonds.

mixed fruit crumble

serves 4

10 minutes

50 minutes

2 mangoes, sliced
1 papaya, seeded and sliced
8 oz/225 g fresh pineapple, cubed
1 1/2 tsp ground ginger
3 1/2 oz/100 g vegetarian margarine
1/2 cup light brown sugar

1 1/8 cups all-purpose flour
generous 3/8 cup dry unsweetened
coconut, plus extra to decorate

Tropical fruits have been used in this crumble, flavored with ginger and coconut, for something a little different and very tasty.

variation

Papayas have an orangey-yellow skin and should yield to gentle pressure.

Use other fruits, such as plums, apples, or blackberries, as a fruit base and add chopped nuts to the topping instead of the coconut.

Preheat the oven to 350°F/180°C. Place the fruit in a pan with 1/2 teaspoon of the ginger, 2 tablespoons of the margarine and 1/4 cup of the sugar. Cook over low heat for 10 minutes, until the fruit softens. Spoon the fruit into the base of a shallow ovenproof dish.

Mix the flour and remaining ginger together in a large bowl. Rub in the remaining margarine until the mixture resembles fine bread crumbs, then stir in the remaining sugar and the coconut. Spoon over the fruit to cover completely.

Cook the crumble in the preheated oven at for 40 minutes, or until the top is crisp. Decorate with coconut and serve.

fall fruit
bread pudding

serves 8

10 minutes

15 minutes

2 lb/900 g mixed blackberries,
    chopped apples, chopped pears
generous ¾ cup light brown sugar
1 tsp ground cinnamon

generous ⅓ cup water
8 oz/225 g white bread,
    thinly sliced, crusts removed

This is like a summer pudding, but it uses fruits which appear later in the year, such as apples, pears, and blackberries, as a succulent filling.

cook's tip

Stand the pudding on a plate when chilling to catch any juices that run down the sides of the bowl.

This pudding would be delicious served with vanilla ice cream to counteract the tartness of the blackberries.

Place the fruit in a large pan with the sugar, cinnamon, and the water, stir, and bring to a boil. Lower the heat and let simmer for 5–10 minutes so that the fruits soften but still hold their shape.

Meanwhile, line the base and sides of an 3½-cup ovenproof bowl with the bread slices, ensuring that there are no gaps between the pieces of bread.

Spoon the fruit into the center of the bread-lined bowl and cover the fruit with the remaining bread.

Place a saucer on top of the bread and weight it down. Let chill in the refrigerator overnight.

Turn the pudding out onto a serving plate and serve at once.

apple fritters & almond sauce

serves 4

15 minutes

15 minutes

scant ⅔ cup all-purpose flour

pinch of salt

½ tsp ground cinnamon, plus extra to decorate

¾ cup warm water

4 tsp vegetable oil

2 egg whites

2 eating apples, peeled

vegetable or corn oil, for deep-frying

superfine sugar, to decorate

sauce

⅔ cup plain yogurt

½ tsp almond extract

2 tsp honey

These apple fritters are coated in a light, spiced batter and deep-fried until crisp and golden. Serve warm.

Sift the flour and salt into a large bowl.

Add the cinnamon and mix well. Stir in the water and oil to form a smooth batter.

Whisk the egg whites in a clean, dry bowl until stiff peaks form, then gently fold into the batter.

Using a sharp knife, cut the apples into chunks and dip the pieces of apple into the batter to coat.

Heat the oil for deep-frying in a heavy-bottom pan to 350°F/180°C, or until a cube of bread browns in 30 seconds. Deep-fry the apple pieces, in batches, for 3–4 minutes, until golden brown and puffy.

Remove the apple fritters from the oil with a slotted spoon and let drain on paper towels.

variation

Use pieces of banana or pineapple instead of the apple, if you prefer.

Mix some superfine sugar and cinnamon together, then sprinkle lightly over the fritters.

Mix all the ingredients for the sauce together in a serving bowl, then serve at once with the fritters.

cherry crêpes

serves 4

10 minutes

15 minutes

filling
14 oz/400 g canned pitted cherries, plus juice
¹/2 tsp almond extract
¹/2 tsp ground allspice
2 tbsp cornstarch

crêpes
scant ²/3 cup all-purpose flour
pinch of salt

2 tbsp chopped fresh mint
1 egg
1¹/4 cups milk
vegetable oil, for cooking

to decorate
confectioners' sugar
toasted slivered almonds

This dish can be made with either fresh pitted cherries or canned cherries for speed.

Place the cherries and 1¼ cups of the juice in a pan with the almond extract and allspice. Stir in the cornstarch and bring to a boil, stirring, until thickened and clear. Set aside until required.

To make the crêpes, sift the flour into a bowl with the salt. Add the chopped mint and make a well in the center. Gradually beat in the egg and milk to form a smooth batter.

Heat 1 tablespoon oil in a 7-inch/18-cm skillet. Pour off the oil when hot. Add just enough batter to coat the bottom of the skillet and cook for 1–2 minutes, or until the underside is cooked. Flip the crêpe over and cook for 1 minute. Remove the crêpe from the skillet and keep warm. Heat another 1 tablespoon of the oil in the skillet and repeat to use up all the batter.

variation
Use other fillings, such as gooseberries or blackberries, as an alternative to the cherries.

Spoon one-quarter of the cherry filling onto a quarter of each crêpe and fold the crêpe into a cone shape. Dust with confectioners' sugar and sprinkle the slivered almonds over the top. Serve.

lemon & lime
syllabus

serves 4

4 hours 15 minutes

–

¼ cup superfine sugar

grated zest and juice of
   1 small lemon

grated zest and juice of
   1 small lime

¼ cup Marsala or medium sherry

1¼ cups heavy cream

lime and lemon zest, to decorate

This dessert is rich, but absolutely delicious. It is not, however, for the calorie conscious as it contains a high proportion of cream, but it's well worth blowing the diet for!

Place the sugar, fruit juices and zest, and Marsala in a bowl, mix well, and let infuse for 2 hours.

Add the cream to the mixture and whisk until it just holds its shape.

Spoon the mixture into 4 tall serving glasses and let chill in the refrigerator for 2 hours.

Decorate with lime and lemon zest and serve.

cook's tip

Serve with almond cookies or uncoated florentines. Do not overwhip the cream when adding to the lemon and lime mixture because it may curdle.

Replace the heavy cream with plain yogurt for a healthier version of this dessert, or use half quantities of both. Whisk the cream before adding to the yogurt.

variation

For an alternative citrus flavor substitute 2 oranges for the lemon and lime, if you prefer.

banana & mango tart

serves 8

1 hour 15 minutes

5 minutes

8-inch/20-cm baked pastry shell
toasted coconut chips, to decorate

filling
2 small ripe bananas
1 mango, sliced
3½ tbsp cornstarch

¼ cup raw brown sugar
1¼ cups soymilk
⅔ cup coconut milk
1 tsp vanilla extract

Bananas and mangoes are a great combination of colors and flavors, especially when topped with toasted coconut chips.

cook's tip

Coconut chips are available in some supermarkets and most health foodstores. It is worth using them as they look much more attractive and are not as sweet as dry unsweetened coconut.

Choose mangoes with shiny and unblemished skins. To test whether they are ripe, gently cup the mango in your hand, and squeeze gently—the mango should yield slightly to the touch.

Slice the bananas and arrange half in the baked pastry shell with half of the mango pieces.

Place the cornstarch and sugar in a pan and mix together. Slowly stir in the soy and coconut milks until combined and cook over low heat, beating until the mixture thickens.

Stir in the vanilla extract, then pour the mixture over the fruit.

Top with the remaining fruit and toasted coconut chips. Let chill in the refrigerator for 1 hour before serving.

chocolate & tofu cheesecake

serves 12

15 minutes

1 hour 15 minutes

5½ oz/150 g vegetarian margarine, plus extra for greasing

scant ⅔ cup all-purpose flour

1 cup ground almonds

1 cup raw brown sugar

1 lb 8 oz/675 g firm tofu (drained weight)

¾ cup vegetable oil

½ cup orange juice

¾ cup brandy

½ cup unsweetened cocoa, plus extra for dusting

2 tsp almond extract

confectioners' sugar, for dusting

cape gooseberries, to decorate

This cheesecake takes a little time to prepare and cook, but is well worth the effort. It is quite rich and is good served or decorated with a little fresh fruit, such as sliced strawberries.

cook's tip

Cape gooseberries make an attractive decoration for many desserts. Peel open the husks to expose the bright orange fruits.

Preheat the oven to 325°F/160°C. Lightly grease and line the base of a 9-inch/23-cm springform cake pan. Place the flour, ground almonds, and 1 tablespoon of the sugar in a bowl and mix well. Rub the margarine into the mixture to form a dough.

Press the dough into the base of the prepared pan to cover, pushing the dough right up to the edge of the pan.

Coarsely chop the tofu and place in a food processor with the remaining ingredients and process until smooth and creamy. Pour over the base in the pan and cook in the preheated oven for 1–1½ hours, or until set.

Let cool in the pan for 5 minutes, then remove from the pan and let chill in the refrigerator. Dust with confectioners' sugar and unsweetened cocoa and decorate with cape gooseberries. Serve.

chocolate fudge pudding

serves 4

10 minutes

40 minutes

1¾ oz/50 g vegetarian margarine, plus extra for greasing

scant ½ cup light brown sugar

2 eggs, beaten

1½ cups milk

scant ½ cup chopped walnuts

scant ⅓ cup all-purpose flour

2 tbsp unsweetened cocoa, plus extra for dusting

confectioners' sugar, for dusting

This dessert has a hidden surprise when cooked as it separates to give a rich chocolate sauce at the bottom of the dish.

Preheat the oven to 350°F/180°C. Lightly grease a 4-cup ovenproof dish.

Cream the margarine and sugar together in a large bowl until fluffy. Beat in the eggs.

Gradually stir in the milk and add the walnuts.

Sift the flour and unsweetened cocoa into the batter and, using a metal spoon, fold in gently until well mixed.

Spoon the batter into the dish and cook in the preheated oven for 35–40 minutes, or until the sponge is cooked.

Dust with confectioners' sugar and unsweetened cocoa and serve.

cook's tip

Serve with sour cream for a luxuriously rich dessert.

variation

Add 1–2 tablespoons brandy or rum to the mixture for a slightly alcoholic dessert, or 1–2 tablespoons orange juice for a child-friendly version.

Index